Leadership Essentials
for Children's Ministry

Passion→Attitude→Teamwork→Honor

by
Craig Jutila

Flagship church resources
from Group Publishing

Group's R.E.A.L. Guarantee to you:

Every Group resource incorporates our R.E.A.L. approach to ministry—
a unique philosophy that results in long-term retention and life
transformation. It's ministry that's:

**This is EARL.
He's R.E.A.L.
mixed up.
(Get it?)**

Relational
Because student-to-
student interaction
enhances learning and
builds Christian
friendships.

Experiential
Because what students
experience sticks with
them up to 9 times
longer than what they
simply hear or read.

Applicable
Because the aim of
Christian education is
to be both hearers and
doers of the Word.

Learner-based
Because students learn
more and retain it
longer when the
process is designed
according to how they
learn best.

Credits
Editor: Gary Wilde
Acquisitions Editor: Karl Leuthauser
Chief Creative Officer: Joani Schultz
Copy Editor: Betty Taylor
Art Director: Sharon Anderson
Computer Graphic Artist: Tracy K. Donaldson
Cover Art Director: Jeff A. Storm
Cover Designer: Alan Furst Inc.
Production Manager: Peggy Naylor

Jutila, Craig, 1965-
    Leadership essentials for children's ministry : passion, attitude, teamwork, honor / by
Craig Jutila.
        p. cm.
    Includes bibliographical references.
    ISBN 0-7644-2389-4 (alk. paper)
    1. Church work with children. 2. Christian leadership. I. Title.
    BV639.C4 J88 2001
    259'.22--dc21

                                                                    2001054846

DEDICATION

This book is dedicated to my family. To my wife, Mary, the second holy spirit in my life: Your encouraging words and energizing heart keep me constantly on the right PATH. Also to my two children, Alec and Cameron, who bring me joy beyond words. My prayer is that I can model to you the right path in life. "A righteous man who walks in his integrity—How blessed are his sons after him" (Proverbs 20:7, New American Standard Bible). I love you.

ACKNOWLEDGMENTS

To Mom and Dad. Thanks for helping me walk the right PATH in life.

To all the leaders at Saddleback. It is an honor to serve with others who have a passion for what they do. We are making a difference!

To my entire staff at Saddleback. What a privilege to serve with a dream team. Phil Jackson never had it this good.

To all of the children's leaders in the world who never give up! Thanks for sustaining and advancing the love of Jesus through your tenacity and leadership.

CONTENTS

Introduction:
Leading Them...*Where?* 5

→Leading Them . . . *Where?*

→Little Jordan wiggles and squirms as he tries to remain seated in his second-grade Sunday school class. Constantly moving, he certainly isn't listening. He's definitely causing distractions. When the teacher asks for the right answer, Jordan is quick with a "creative" response that's a bit off-color. The other kids roar with laughter.

On this particular day, Jordan is exceptionally energetic. He spent the night at his dad's new house, and Mom forgot to send Jordan's prescribed medication for his ADD. After one of his many outbursts, Jordan's teacher asks him to sit quietly, away from the other children. *Seems like he needs to be on medication—or something,* his teacher thinks as she escorts him over to the time-out corner.

→Each Sunday as Mandy comes to church, she likes to sit and play with one particular doll. She's said maybe three words in the past several weeks. Most of the teachers think she's just shy, but there's a story behind Mandy's silence. Her mom has told her, "Daddy won't be living with us anymore."

Silent Mandy.

Yet three months ago, she'd stolen the show at her dance recital, singing and dancing better than any other kindergartner. Now she whispers to her favorite doll, "Daddy's moving out, but don't be sad, Lila..."

→Sean enters his fifth-grade classroom and glances over at a group of guys and girls gathered in the far corner. Immediately some of them begin pointing and smirking. Sean points back, shouting loudly. After class, he pushes one of the boys and shoves his way outside. "You don't know my life!" is Sean's only offering when one of the leaders follows him.

Then a car pulls up to the curb, and a gravelly voice sounds in the air, "Get your rear in the car! We're late." Sean's entire body tenses as he walks away. He jerks open the car door and sinks into the front seat, looking down the whole time.

Do you recognize these kids? No doubt you have a few Jordans, Mandys, and Seans sitting in your own classrooms and programs every week. And I believe you picked up this book because you want to ensure that they'll begin to fare a little better in the future than they have in the past. In other words, you want to lead them onto pathways that make for good and joyful days ahead. You also know that your own leadership skills—and your ability to develop excellent leadership in others—will make all the difference for those children.

Where Are They Headed?

One of the things determining how well our children thrive is the quality of planning and leading we adults do on their behalf. Each year in our children's ministry at Saddleback Church, we focus on a theme. I launch this theme each year by taking our children's staff to Palm Springs—in August. If you know anything about Palm Springs in August, you know that the temperature can reach 115 degrees in the shade. (But you can get a really nice hotel room for a dollar—so, we go in August.) At that retreat, we launch our yearly theme. Some of the past themes have been "No Plateaus," "A Rising Tide," and the theme this book is based on, "Leading on the Right PATH." For our theme verse, I chose

> **Trust in the Lord with all your heart, and lean not on your own understanding; in all your ways acknowledge him, and he will make your paths straight.**—Proverbs 3:5-6

The New Century Version (NCV) says, "Remember the Lord in all you do, and he will give you success." In our planning session, I focused on this gem of scriptural wisdom and suggested an acrostic for leadership success that follows the letters in PATH:

P for passion,
A for attitude,
T for teamwork, and
H for honor.

It's interesting that during the four years I crammed into five at Biola University, I never attended a class dealing with these four areas. Don't get me wrong, I had stellar educators and teachers and the education I received there was fantastic. However, the four areas we'll explore in this book concerning effective leadership for a dynamic ministry are rarely taught in universities. Nevertheless, they are critical to the success of your children's ministry: passion, attitude, teamwork, and honor. This simple formula keeps our children's staff focused and helps us function together as an effective team. Each member has an individual personality, yet we lead together toward common goals and common initiatives—and have fun while doing it. I believe the approach leads to success because it's clearly supported by Scripture:

Passion

When there's ministry work to do, we can either approach it as a boring chore or as an energizing act of worship:

In all the work you are doing, work the best you can. Work as if you were doing it for the Lord, not for people. —Colossians 3:23, NCV

Attitude

Our mind-set will determine our level of happiness and satisfaction within any ministry:

Be full of joy in the Lord always. I will say again, be full of joy. —Philippians 4:4, NCV

Teamwork

We can always be more effective if we avoid a lone-ranger approach and link up with others whose gifts can support and complement our own:

Two people are better than one. They get more done by working together. If one person falls, the other can help him up. But it is bad for the person who is alone when he falls...A rope that has three parts wrapped together is hard to break. —Ecclesiastes 4:9-12, International Children's Bible

Honor

Serving in an atmosphere of mutual respect and encouragement makes any ministry enjoyable and worth all the effort:

Love each other like brothers and sisters. Give each other more honor than you want for yourselves. —Romans 12:10, NCV

It's my firm belief that following these four signposts of healthy ministry leadership will help us travel a straight path toward success. But note that God didn't say a "clear" path or a "no pothole" path. Nor did he say where the path would incline uphill or where the lights would shine brightly upon it. God simply promised the path would be "straight," as we walk along trusting in him.

My hope and prayer is that this book will serve as a catalyst for creative thinking, a new paradigm, or perhaps a reminder of why we are in this thing called children's ministry, a ministry that should always be conducted on the right PATH. So let's lead our Jordans, Mandys, Seans—and all the children and volunteers in our ministries— along that blessed pathway.

PASSION

PART ONE

*"**f**orgetting the past and looking forward to what lies ahead, I strain to reach the end of the race and receive the prize for which God, through Christ Jesus, is calling us up to heaven."*

—Philippians 3:13b-14, New Living Translation

ONE

→Losing Your Breath Is Better Than Losing Your Mind

"Take five laps, guys!"

It was another end-of-training-day marathon. The laps encompassed the entire ball field, and every player strained to come in first. When I finally crawled back to the locker room, the sweat poured down my forehead as I gasped for air.

Some people say baseball players aren't necessarily the fittest athletes, despite their spectacular coordination and perfectly honed finesse. But I beg to differ about the physical conditioning. After four years of college baseball, I can attest to some pretty strenuous workouts.

Now, coming back to the locker room after another race for home plate, I gulped for oxygen—and thought about *breathing*. In fact, as I played baseball through college, whenever I went back to my locker, I saw a verse I had taped to my locker when I was a freshman. For four years I stared at this Scripture:

Whatever you do, work at it with all your heart, as working for the Lord, not for men. —Colossians 3:23

At the time, this verse compelled me to success. Not success as in "Did you win the game?" "Did you come out on top?" or "Did you defeat your opponent?" No, this verse caused me to think about *inner* success. The questions I had to ask myself every day for four years were "Craig, did you give it your best?" "Did you lose your breath on this one?" and "Did you do it for your Savior?" This verse doesn't tell us to win; it tells us to give our best, give it our all. Why? Because God deserves it.

After I graduated, I did a more in-depth word study on that verse, focusing on "best you can." In the original Greek, this phrase is *ek psuche*. It may be translated "out of soul" or "out of breath." So, "in all the work you're doing, do it with all of your soul"—or *"out of breath" with passion*.

Let Your Passion *Produce*

> We need passion because we just can't live without what it *produces*.

Breathless! You can look at a passionate person and almost see the need for a little more air than the rest of us require. The passionate people are so "into" what they're doing that they may well be out of breath.

Breathless with dedication to God's calling.

Absolutely gasping with spiritual inspiration and vitality.

I have seen too many children's workers "doing ministry" because "no one else was doing it" and the "job" needed to get done. Some of them have even said, "I'm doing this part time until they can get someone in here and take care of these kids. I don't even like kids."

Listen, I know all of us found our way into children's ministry one way or another. Some were called, some were chosen. I was dragged—listless, apathetic, and downright protesting. I told the senior associate pastor at my church that I would "do it" (children's ministry) for six months, but they'd better start looking for someone else ASAP. I didn't want to work with kids; I had no experience with kids. In fact, I was so inexperienced that when I read "Up to 8 lbs" on those diaper packages, I thought that's how much the diaper held. But God changed my heart. How? It's my approach to life in general. Whatever I do, I do it well because I am doing it for God, not for the approval of others.

This is the kind of passion I'm inviting you to nurture in your own life—for the best of ministry, for the most effective leadership, for the ultimate in leadership team development, not merely for the sake of making a change. No, we need passion because we just can't live without what it *produces*. Let's look at some of its fruits.

I. Passion Produces Drive.

It's the octane for the tank, the gas for the car. When people run out of it we say, "Boy, they're really apathetic, listless, unconcerned." With passion, we have the enthusiasm for pushing ahead. With passion, we have the energy to drive through to the finish line of accomplishment.

I think the apostle Paul was just this type of person. How else could he have penned words like these:

> **I do all this for the sake of the Good News in order to share what it offers. Don't you realize that everyone who runs in a race runs to win, but only one runner gets the prize? Run like them, so that you can win. Everyone who enters an athletic contest goes into strict training. They do it to win a temporary crown, but we do it to win one that will be permanent. So I run—but not without a clear goal ahead of me. So I box—but not as if I were just shadow boxing. Rather, I toughen my body with punches and make it my slave so that I will not be disqualified after I have spread the Good News to others.**
> —I Corinthians 9:23-27, God's Word Translation

(passion)

Paul was out of breath with running to witness, training to reach Christian maturity, and straining to win the reward. The bottom line—it's not unchristian to have some drive! In fact, it's essential.

2. Passion Produces Possibilities.

The Bible says, "With God, all things are possible." We have to make room to say, "God doesn't fit inside our little box of the possible." God will give you something to do in your life, whether it's children's ministry or something else you can't do on your own. Why does he do this? If we could accomplish the work with our own resources alone, why would we need God to show up? For us to be stretched and God to be glorified, we need to be thrust into impossible situations, situations in which he needs to show up for things to work. That's why the Bible says,

> *If we could accomplish the work with our own resources alone, why would we need God to show up?*

As far as possibilities go, everything is possible for the person who believes. —Mark 9:23b, GWT

With a passion that believes in the power of God, the possibilities are endless. Therefore, the passionate person does things a little differently from the apathetic observers sitting on the sidelines of life:

➜A passionate person overcomes difficulties in life. Rather than opting out of the race at the first sign of difficulty, he or she seeks creative solutions in tandem with others.

➜A passionate person crashes through the quitting points by viewing failure as a steppingstone to success. These folks keep setting new goals, and they achieve them through perseverance.

➜A passionate person accepts challenges that push to the limits of endurance. Instead of interpreting tough trials as dangerous threats to their well-being, they realize, "No pain, no gain." And if the Lord disciplines them, they learn to accept it as a precious demonstration of God's love.

So what are your passions? What are the possibilities God has started swirling around in your mind—the things he envisions for your ministry as you put that passion to work for him?

My two greatest passions are seeing a child come to Christ and then growing that child toward spiritual maturity. I'm equally passionate about seeing volunteers give their time with joyful hearts. It is my passion to lead them, encourage them, build them up in every way, and inspire them to see the visions for ministry that God lays out before them. In other words, my passion is to significantly touch and build into their lives, on the kid level and on the adult level. But what is it for you?

Increase Passion by Building Ownership

One of the ways you can spark passion within your ministry team, among your volunteers, and even throughout your entire congregation is by concentrating on building a sense of ownership. When everyone "takes it personally"—deeply identifies with the mission, the vision, the methods, and the other members of the team—then the passion floodgates will open wide. The simple truth is that we *really care* about those things that we feel are part of us. We take personal responsibility for those things, and we become passionate about them. We want those things to "be the best," because they reflect on us.

Building ownership in your children's ministry will be an ongoing task, because it normally develops slowly, over time. It increases as people find that their voice matters and their attempts to influence the direction of the ministry have good effect. Thus they begin to see their importance to the ministry—and the ministry, in turn, becomes more important to them. After all, they have invested their time, energy, and creative thinking. They don't want their efforts wasted!

If you'd like to begin assessing the levels of ownership on your team, take some time at your next meeting to answer questions like the ones below. (Note: Photocopy and distribute this assessment to the team members a week in advance. Give everyone a chance to jot responses they can bring to a discussion time.)

Do I have a sense of ownership in this ministry?

Instructions: Check one of the words on the scale to indicate your response to each statement. Then be ready to share and explain your thoughts in your team meeting.

1. I feel completely free to speak up and voice my opinion in our meetings here.

     ❑ Never   ❑ Rarely   ❑ Sometimes   ❑ Usually   ❑ Always

Explaining my response:

_____

_____

2. I know my skills, contributions, and opinions are highly valued here.

     ❑ Never   ❑ Rarely   ❑ Sometimes   ❑ Usually   ❑ Always

Explaining my response:

_____

_____

3. I feel a sense of anticipation and enthusiasm when asked to carry out a task in this ministry.

❏ Never ❏ Rarely ❏ Sometimes ❏ Usually ❏ Always

Explaining my response:

_____

_____

4. I have always felt that I was an important player when it comes to setting the goals and objectives for this ministry.

❏ Never ❏ Rarely ❏ Sometimes ❏ Usually ❏ Always

Explaining my response:

_____

_____

5. I tend to be at the forefront of activity when it comes to implementing our plans in this ministry.

❏ Never ❏ Rarely ❏ Sometimes ❏ Usually ❏ Always

Explaining my response:

_____

_____

6. I enjoy a deep sense of satisfaction through participating in this group and this ministry.

❏ Never ❏ Rarely ❏ Sometimes ❏ Usually ❏ Always

Explaining my response:

_____

_____

Debriefing Suggestion:

If you've heard few "usually" or "always" statements during your discussion, you'll want to work on ownership issues. But don't attempt any problem solving at this meeting. Simply appoint a note taker who will recap several key problem or conflict areas raised in the discussion. Then your group can plan to deal with these, one by one, in future team meetings. ■

3. Passion Produces Life Change.

As a result of having passion in your life, you will do things you wouldn't ordinarily do if you were apathetic. When you see the world through passionate eyes, you see things enhanced or magnified. Flowers smell better, the sky looks brighter, and the horizon of life looks so much more promising.

That kind of change produces a tough-minded commitment. Recently, I was in the middle of a conference in Texas and I made the unfortunate mistake of mentioning Texas football. Texas folks are just out of control about college athletics—especially college football! I happened to be in the wrong town, and I mentioned the Texas Longhorns. I had a hundred people booing me before I said another word.

So I quickly became a Texas A&M fan.

Now they all loved me! But I didn't really explore the depths of A&M passion until one of my staff members, Cynthia Petty, told me about the traditions of football at A&M.

"Craig," she said. "You have to understand something about Aggie football."

"What's that?"

"When the student body and alumni go to the game, they stand during the whole game."

"You've got to be kidding!"

"No, from the time they walk in, they never take a seat."

I couldn't believe it. "But that's nuts!" I said.

"Listen, Craig," she replied. "I had my kids home not too long ago when the Aggies were playing. They couldn't go to the game, so they watched it on television."

I thought, *Well, what's the big deal about that?*

"Craig, they stood in the living room for every minute of that game—even during the commercials."

Now that's passion. It doesn't matter what other people think of them. They have it, their lives are transformed by it, and they're going to stand up for it.

Will you? Will you stand up for your leaders? Will you stand up for the kids in your ministry? Will you let passion influence your life to bring about Kingdom difference? Hey, if thirty thousand Texas students can get excited for three hours a week watching twenty-two men chase a brown piece of leather, you would think that those of us who serve in children's ministry can muster up some energy about the spiritual growth of kids. In fact, why wouldn't our enthusiasm for those kids put a football crowd to shame?

Are you with me?

How Will You Know You've Got It?

You might be thinking, *Well, Craig, this is all very inspiring, but right now I'm just trying to survive in ministry.* If that's where you are, I'd like to ask you to place your feelings of frustration and despair aside for awhile until you can read through the first three chapters of this book. Passion is something you must choose. It may take a bit of courage at this point in your life. So, for the moment, just forge ahead with me and begin to embrace the qualities of the passionate person, one small step at a time.

(passion)

Here is a principle I've been taught: You need to *act your way into feeling, not feel your way into acting.* If we were to feel our way into acting, nothing would ever get done. Most of us would never get up, and all of us would live in Hawaii.

What are those special characteristics of a passionate person? When you're looking for passion, the evidence will show up in all the E's people display:

→Excitement and Energy

You can identify passionate people even from their nonverbal communication. They can walk into a room, and the energy level in that room changes.

Whenever I have a chance to speak to children's pastors or leaders in the ministry, the one thing they often say to me is, "I really appreciate the energy you bring to the ministry." If I go speak to a specific ministry, my listeners may miss the total content of the presentation, but they always say, "Great energy, Craig!" You can go a long way with the energy of passion. Passion is the edge that takes the average performer and turns her into an extraordinary one. That's why I will always hire a passionate person over an intelligent, apathetic person. This is what I know: You can't steer a parked car, you can't navigate a floating boat, and you can't coach an apathetic person. Why? Because they are not *moving.*

> Passion is the edge that takes the average performer and turns her into an extraordinary one.

One day I was driving home from church, really exhausted, as I had just finished "one of those days." I thought to myself, *As soon as I get home, I'm going to the fridge, grab a root beer, order up a pizza, and just veg. I'll tell the pizza guy that the door will be open. I'm not moving. I'm going to get the remote, flip on ESPN, and watch the Kings game for the next three hours. I am not even going to get up to answer the phone.*

That was my plan. I got home, ordered the pizza, got my drink, took the remote, and switched on ESPN.

Then the phone rang. *I mean it, I am not moving.* Even if the house were on fire, I would have waited until it burned right up to my feet. I am glued to the chair. Get the picture?

I have to tell you at this point that I'm a big hockey fan. I love going to the games in person, love hearing the *zing* of steel on ice, love feeling the jolt of those bone-crunching body checks up against the glass. Anyway, I hear my friend say on the answering machine, "Craig, I know you're home, and I've got a couple of King's tickets—on the glass."

"On the glass"—my three favorite words—the best seats in the house. Ironically, I found myself not only out of the chair but burning down the hallway to the answering machine, as well. I can remember diving across our bed and knocking the phone off the table just to let my friend know I was there.

"Do you have tickets for the King's game on the glass?" I asked.

"Yes," he said. "Right behind the bench."

My friend was on his way to my house. I quickly changed from my sweats to the appropriate home-team colors and hat, grabbed a sweatshirt, and was on my way outside as my friend turned the corner to my street. In synchronous motion, he slowed down as I jumped into the car, and we were off. Now that is passion at its energetic best! We passed the pizza guy coming around the corner.

This story should give you hope. I want you to see that passion is a choice—your choice. Try it out next Sunday. Try it out when your alarm goes off and you roll over and think, *I don't want to go to church today; little Zachary is going to be there.*

Instead say, "*Wow!* Today is a great day because I am going to choose to be excited about life and ministry. And unlike anybody else in this world today, I get to minister to little Zachary. In fact, I hope he's at church early today!"

That's acting your way into feeling. That's making the right choice. That's getting excited about making a Kingdom difference because what we do will last forever, not just until the end of a third period, a fourth quarter, or a ninth inning.

The evidence of passion will be energy, and it springs from a heart choice, not just a head choice. In other words, are you close to Jesus these days? When you are, the *things* of Jesus, the things of his kingdom, will send jolts of passion into your soul every time you have the opportunity to be part of the game. On that exhausting day, I chose to let my excitement flow.

→Enthusiasm and Expectancy

Here are two more qualities of passionate people. We get our word *enthusiasm* from the biblical Greek word *entheos, En* meaning *within*, and *theos* meaning *God*. So *enthusiasm* means *within God*. As we minister to kids and within our families, we should be the most enthusiastic people of all, because we are living our lives within the boundaries of God's love, grace, and power.

Living within God means we've let him lead us into our particular vocation, our particular place, and the particular type of work he wants us to do. If that's the case, how could we fail to be enthusiastic and expectant? We're doing what we do because we are in line with his will for our lives. I like the way one twentieth-century poet put it:

A student at work on his true vocation becomes creative and passionate. A professional whose work comes out of his very soul should almost have to pay instead of being paid for doing that which fills his life with light. Doing things out of obligation, no matter how much effort you put into it, will always be like dragging a ball and chain. Because of this, every[one] should struggle to love what he does when he cannot do what he loves.
—J. L. Martin Descalzo[1]

When you're near passionate people, who love what they do, you're just waiting for things to happen. Did you hear that? You're waiting for things to happen. You're not standing around to see *if* something will happen, because you know something *will* happen. It could be something totally off the wall, out of the box, just kind of nuts. But something is going to happen, because passion is characterized by enthusiasm and expectancy.

(passion)

> The kids may not remember a lesson you teach, but they'll remember *who you are.*

→Exceptional Effects

The bottom line is that awesome spiritual results blossom from our passion in ministry. If you come in, week after week, to teach kids or carry out other ministries, and it's just the same monotony, the same old thing...well, it's tough.

But imagine approaching your task with passion—passion for the great privilege you've been granted. Kids will catch your enthusiasm, volunteers will grasp the vision, and ministry will be vital. The kids may not remember a lesson you teach, but they'll remember *who you are.* They will remember you as a passionate person who loved them and valued them and honored them—one who came to them with energy and excitement, expecting exceptional things to happen in the group every week.

Is Your Ministry to Children Worth Your Oxygen?

Despite all I'm inviting you to do, I realize it isn't particularly easy to live with passion; it calls for giving up something very important to us. Here's what I mean: A man once said that when it comes to passion, "It's not the *mountain* we conquer but *ourselves.*"

Who uttered that profound truth? It was Sir Edmund Hillary, the first person to climb Mount Everest along with his Sherpa friend, Tenzing Norgay, in 1953. Hillary, of all people, certainly knew that mountains weren't easy to conquer!

Let's think about this for a moment. First, how much do you know about Mount Everest? For example,

→it's the tallest mountain in the world, looming 29,035 feet—five and a half miles above sea level;

→it swirls with blizzards of 100-mile-an-hour winds and 100-below-zero wind-chills;

→it has lured over 4,000 people to attempt climbing its peak;

→it has allowed only about 700 to make it (paying about $70,000 each); and

→it has claimed the lives of more than 140 climbers.

Once Edmund Hillary began his expedition, it took seven weeks—and 400 helpers—to reach the top. Various stops at base camps along the way helped the climbers stabilize to the decreasing oxygen levels. Food at the higher altitudes becomes repugnant, so for the final days, Hillary consumed a weak, lukewarm tea spiked with loads of sugar. During the entire three-day ascent up the sheer incline of the final 800 feet, sleep, too, was virtually impossible.

Everest's peak thrusts into the sky at more than 29,000 feet, but when Hillary reached the 25,000-foot mark, he entered what is known as "the death zone." At that altitude, the air is so thin that breathing it begins to impair normal bodily functions. In fact, oxygen depletion can become so severe that it kills, even as the victim continues to breathe with some degree of apparent normality. At best, oxygen depletion can severely hamper the judgment of a climber—as if he or she had taken a large dose of sedative.

> Was today
> worth losing
> my breath?

In other words, fellow children's minister, *it will be grueling for us to attempt to conquer all the obstacles in our path to ministry success.* Most bothersome are the things within us that try to pull us down when we want to create a spirit of unity and passion within our ministry teams.

To reach the summit, we'll need to be willing to lose our breath—willing to become breathless with our passion to reach the pinnacle of God's vision for our lives.

Often I need a reminder that what I am doing really matters. Was today worth losing my breath? In my office, I've placed daily reminders of *why* I'm passionate:

→a vision statement on the wall reminding me of why our children's ministry exists;

→a broken mug with a picture of eight kids on it, representing my first mission trip with a group of children some ten years ago;

→a box of toys and knickknacks that my staff gave me last year, each lifting up some aspect of leadership in my life that had touched theirs; and

→pictures of several eagles, each reminding me of Isaiah 40:31:
   But the people who trust the Lord will become strong again. They will rise up as an eagle in the sky; they will run and not need rest; they will walk and not become tired. —New Century Version

The trusting people will stay strong because they breathe on the Lord's terms and give up their right to grab their own oxygen, trusting him for the daily supply of everything they need. Remember,
   In all the work you do,
   Do it with all of your breath,
   With passion.

(passion)

For Reflection and Discussion

1. What is your favorite hobby? Do you approach ministry with as much passion as you do your hobby?

2. Who is a good example of a passionate person in your life? What have you learned from this person?

3. Think about the three "fruits" of passion. Which seems most needed in your ministry team or church these days? for yourself?

4. To what extent have you been inspired to become more passionate about children's ministry? What are some next steps to take?

5. Make a list of the things your group can be excited and enthused about as you approach the year ahead. What spiritual "effects," or results, can you expect from your passion?

Endnote

1. J. L. Martin Descalzo, in Reader's Digest, as quoted in Gary Wilde, *All Preachers Great and Small: A Pastor's Appreciation Book* (Wheaton, IL: Harold Shaw Publishers, 1996), 56-57.

TWO

→Has Your Passion Paused?

"Don't ever let me catch you singing like that again, without enthusiasm," he said. "You're nothing if you aren't excited by what you're doing."[1]

Today, if a dad spoke like that to his son, we would call that statement a good example of poor parenting.

Nevertheless, in the case of Frank Sinatra Jr., apparently these words from his dad had a powerful effect. We do know that young Frank developed a real passion for singing—and he has kept at it for decades.

Not all of us are so blessed to have a never-flagging enthusiasm for our ministry. In some ways, it's simply a sign of the times. We have increased our apathy and reduced our passion. At the risk of "going overboard" or becoming "fanatical"—about anything—many of us have come to believe that if we're just average, we're excelling. And perhaps in an attempt to escape that obvious untruth, we give ourselves over to entertainment and amusement as much as possible. After all, our amusements seem to salve so many of our symptoms of dissatisfaction. Why? Just consider the roots of the word "amusement" itself:

a = not
muse = think

So when we go to an "amusement park," we go to "not think." We assume we can avoid the pain of our apathy by just avoiding our own thoughts.

Beware the Deadly Passion Poisoners

But to know all of this about apathy may not be very helpful to you right now. After all, you may be suffering a serious attack of indifference these days, through a loss of direction or as a result of good, old-fashioned overwork. Or you may face a staff or group of volunteers who can't seem to get motivated for their ministries, no matter how much you preach and cajole. One thought to consider is this: I always say that most things are caught, not taught. And this is very true with passion. If you have an apathetic team, you first may need to check your own passion gauge.

Let me suggest that your first step is to analyze exactly what's going on when the workers in the harvest seem more like sleepers in the field. This chapter will do that quick diagnosis. The next chapter will offer some practical prescriptions for revitalizing sanctified passion once again—in yourself and in those you lead. But for now, consider the top five reasons people lose their passion. We might call them "passion poisoners." If people were self-aware enough, honest enough, and courageous enough to admit they were reeling under the influence of these damaging toxins, here's what they'd likely say:

→Passion Poison I: Familiarity

"I guess I'm just so used to the same old routines that I've gotten stuck in a box of monotony, low expectations, and lack of creativity." You've heard the statement "Familiarity breeds contempt." That's really true. Actually, my staff and I talk about this regularly. And we constantly push ourselves to look at everything in new and creative ways. Because if something becomes familiar, apathy starts to set in, we get careless, and we get stuck in a box. As a result, our ministry to the children suffers.

So we try to think *outside* of the box.

Is it time for you to do something that's out of the ordinary for you, maybe with your kids, in your family, or in your ministry? We don't want "Death by Sameness" chiseled on the gravestone of our passion!

Just about every other month, I take my staff on an OOTB event, an "Out of the Box" experience. My staff doesn't know what we're going to do until right before we do it. The day is preselected, but the event remains secret. I simply tell them the time we're leaving, when we'll be back, and what to wear. We have raced cars, gone on a scavenger hunt at the mall, had lunch and games at Dave and Buster's, attended a high tea (my favorite—*not*), painted, sculpted, and caught a few rides at an amusement park.

Early on, we had some staff members who did *not* want to do these OOTB kinds of things. They would rather have stayed at the church and "worked." Little did they know, they *were* working—building a staff family, creating a catalyst for innovation, and renewing passion by, well, just being with one another. Proverbs 27:17 says,

Iron sharpens iron, and one person sharpens the wits of another. —New Revised Standard Version

And what about problems in our ministry? We actually call them "opportunities." Are you still trying to solve them in the same old ways? Are there any other approaches open to you? Take some time to think. Or just let your mind wander through some wild and crazy possibilities as you ponder: *What is the answer here?*

Take a couple of minutes to work on your own creative problem-solving skills by tackling these brain teasers. See whether you can let yourself think outside of the box for awhile! (You'll find the answers at the end of this chapter—but don't peek until you've given it your best effort).

---

1. In your cellar, there are three light switches in the "off" position. Each switch controls one of three light bulbs on the floor above. You may move any of the switches, but you may only go upstairs one time to inspect the bulbs. How can you figure out which bulb goes to which switch if you only get to go upstairs once?

2. Jackie likes indigo but not blue. She likes onions but not turnips; she likes forms but not shapes. According to the same rule, does she like tomatoes or avocados?

3. A wealthy man tells his two sons to race their camels to a distant city to see which son will inherit his fortune. The one whose camel is slower will win. The brothers, after wandering aimlessly for days, ask a wise man for advice. After hearing the advice, they jump on the camels and race as fast as they can to the city. What does the wise man say?

How did you do? I hope this little exercise reminded you that sometimes we need to sit with our problems for awhile and let the sameness of our thinking patterns fade into the background. Then we can see new ways of doing things, new ways of thinking, new ways of accomplishing the vision God has laid before us. Remember, the best way to *think* out of the box is to *move* out of the box. That's why you may need to go to the mall to solve the programming issue you're now facing in your ministry. Please don't let the idea that "We've always done it that way" poison your passion!

→Passion Poison 2: Coolness

"Apparently, I've been isolated—or just hanging out with the wrong people." The Bible tells us that "bad company corrupts good character" (I Corinthians 15:33). We occasionally find ourselves losing passion because we are, in fact, spending the majority of our time with apathetic people. Proverbs 13:20 says, "Whoever walks with wise people will be wise, but whoever associates with fools will suffer" (GWT).

I love to barbecue. When we have great weather here in southern California, I like to 'cue it up a bit and throw a couple of burgers on, or a nice juicy steak.

My father-in-law gave me a Weber barbecue several years ago. The barbecue has a basket at the bottom of the grill that holds the charcoal, allowing each individual piece to be positioned strategically for the best cooking. On this particular July day, one of the brightly glowing coals fell out of the basket into the bottom of the barbecue. I didn't want to pick it up with my hand, so I just let it lie there. When I came back in about ten minutes to put the meat on the grill, I noticed that the coal had slowly fallen apart. It had stopped burning and was just sitting off to the side, cool as a cucumber.

(passion)

It reminded me of the company we keep. When we remove ourselves from passionate people or a passionate team, we're like that coal. We grow cold toward the things of the kingdom. We don't feel the fire anymore, and we gradually isolate ourselves, cool off, and fall apart. To keep the passion burning bright, we need to watch the company we keep and choose to stay around passionate people.

In children's ministry, this means taking the lead in demonstrating enthusiasm and energy for what we do. It means being thoroughly interested in the children and their spiritual growth. Such attitudes are contagious; before long we find ourselves attracting co-workers with similar levels of energy and zeal.

→Passion Poison 3: Uncertainty

> Our focus is extremely important; if we have nothing to live for, it really doesn't matter how long our lives are.

"Maybe I've got the wrong focus—or no focus at all!" Without focus, there's no reason to get up in the morning. It's just another nine-to-five day, or another Sunday, depending on when you're doing ministry. Our focus is extremely important; if we have nothing to live for, it really doesn't matter how long our lives are. So we have to choose—especially when we're investing in kids—to say, "My focus is *here, with them,* bringing them to the Lord and growing them spiritually."

We had just finished a conference at our church in which I had spent a solid hour talking about the calling of God and sticking with that calling. I was relating it to children's ministry by saying that some of us in children's ministry don't look at it as a long-term, settled gig. Instead, we're *moving...*

Moving up—"I am on my way to the top—senior pastor."

Moving over—"This is not for me, but at least it got me 'in.'"

Moving on—"I've done my time; I'm out of jail now."

Moving out—"I quit. This is not for me."

Are you a mover—up, over, on, or out? There may be legitimate reasons to pursue a different calling. But if you know this is where you ought to be, then be passionate about your calling and reject vagueness. Why? Because as our senior pastor, Rick Warren, says, "Nothing becomes dynamic until it becomes specific." In other words, speaking in generalities doesn't help a team accomplish its goals. When we get down to talking about specific steps, specific plans, and specific schedules, then we begin moving forward. It's true with an idea and with ministry and leadership, as well.

After the conference, my staff and some of the folks from my "divine calling" session went to lunch at the food court by our church. When we sat down to eat, one of the women began telling her story. "Not much is going on at my church," she said. "Really, I'm doing all I can, but I never see any results."

I turned and pointedly shot this question at her: "So, what are you going to be doing in the next five years?"

Assessing the Passion Levels

Do you have a truly passionate team, with members who constantly outdo one another in enthusiasm and energy for children's ministry? Or have the "poisoners" infected you to some extent?

Even the best of teams can occasionally feel the sting of the five toxins listed in this chapter. To assess the passion levels in your team means asking some tough questions—and determining to listen with an open mind and open heart. The questions below can help get you started. Be sure to stay focused on the positive solutions available when your problems and concerns have been fully aired.

Are We Poisoning Our Passion Around Here?

Instructions: Choose A, B, or C below, depending on the types of statements you typically hear (or *would* hear if people voiced their genuine feelings) within your team or congregation.

1. Familiarity: *How are the creativity levels these days?*

___ A. "I'm excited; I wonder how we're going to do it this time!"

___ B. "I just wish we had a little predictability in our programming!"

___ C. "But that's the way we've *always* done it."

How I'd like it to be:

_____

_____

2. Coolness: What's the positivity-negativity ratio in our environment?

___ A. "Hey, Gang, let's just spend some time affirming one another before we get started on this meeting."

___ B. "Phone for you, John, line 1—another complainer..."

___ C. "So ends another children's ministry event—what a downer that was!"

How I'd like it to be:

_____

_____

3. Uncertainty: Are we focused—or not?

___ A. "Look! We've met some of our yearly goals these past three months!"

___ B. "Did you turn in your leader roster yet?"

___ C. "There's plenty of time to plan the skits, John—a whole ten minutes before class time....Now where did that fake beard go?"

How I'd like it to be:

_____

_____

4. Rambling: Are the goals clear to everyone?

____ A. "Jennifer just asked me, 'What would Jesus do?' I thought that was a real step of growth for her."

____ B. "Hey, my kids always stay quiet and in their chairs, for the whole hour. What more could I ask?"

____ C. "Now that we've got the kids gathered, let's spend some time outside looking at cloud shapes—or do you prefer finger painting?"

How I'd like it to be:

_____

_____

5. Hardness: Who's hurting—and why?

____ A. "People around here are great about keeping their criticisms as constructive and helpful as possible."

____ B. "Oh no! Oh no! Pastor Bill wants to 'have a little chat' with me about last night's 'Wreck-a-Thon'!"

____ C. "Ouch! I feel like I was just stabbed in the heart with an ice pick—a really dull one."

How I'd like it to be:

_____

_____

Debriefing Suggestion:

This exercise should give you a good idea of what the "corporate climate" is in your team or church. Get together with your team to talk about your responses. As specific issues surface, brainstorm together some of the ways you could release the passion in each of the five areas. Listen to every idea before choosing by consensus a few of the best options! ∎

The question seemed to surprise her. "I don't know," she said. "But I'm thinking of going into missions and working with adults."

"Then why are you working with kids *now*?"

No response. A blank stare. But I had a sneaking suspicion that we had identified the problem at her church with one simple question.

Think it over. What is your lifelong focus? Are you simply doing a job, or are you living out your calling? If it's the latter, then focus your energy. Please don't use children's ministry as a stepping stone to climb some virtual ladder of a church organizational chart. If you are *called* to do children's ministry, then be like Nike and *just do it.*

→Passion Poison 4: Rambling

"If I knew what I wanted to do, maybe I could get excited about it." Similar to having no focus is the unhappy situation of being in ministry with no goals. Yet goals are a prerequisite to having focus in life, because without goals, you have nothing to focus on!

If you have no goals for your life, your family, or your ministry, I will guarantee you one thing: You'll hit those goals every time. You don't need fuel in the tank at this point, because you don't even have a car to get you there. Certainly passion is the fuel for the tank, but you've got to have that car in place. Vince Lombardi, the great Green Bay football coach, said, "The harder you work, the harder it is to surrender."[2] I think that's true. The passion that goes into our ministry and the kids who we minister to is very important. When we invest that passion in specific, doable goals, and work at them with all our God-given strength, then it's harder to give up on our ministry.

When Helen Keller was asked what could be worse than being born blind, she responded, "To have sight without vision."[3] Is that where you are at the moment, seeing but not really envisioning? Why not put this book aside for a moment, and on a separate sheet of paper (or in your journal), prayerfully write down some of your goals for your ministry. Think long and hard about each entry. Consider what will be required for each goal and what interim steps will take you to completion. Then pray, pray, pray for God's leading and power to see things through.

Each year in August, our children's staff lists ten goals or initiatives that we would like to accomplish during the year ahead. We track these goals. We pursue these goals with relentless energy. The decisions we make throughout the year about how to use our resources are prompted by these goals. We talk about them constantly, pray about them, and focus on them. At the end of the year, we sit down and evaluate our performance. How did we do? ten out of ten? eight out of ten? five out of ten? Even if it's five out of ten, that's .500 in baseball (and if you batted .500 in the big leagues, you would make 10 million dollars a year). Pat your team on the back! You hit .500 this year in ministry! That's five times more than another team that had no goals.

Offer your vision to God, making sure it has flowed from his heart into yours. Stay in constant dialogue with God, that his Spirit may lead you each day, as you move forward in his will. Maybe you can't yet thoroughly articulate your vision. If not, simply ask God to lead you onto a special pathway for your ministry. Say, "I'm open, Lord. Show me the way." Then go ahead and set up some goals. Get moving, and trust God to steer you as you go.

(passion)

Passion Poison 5: Hardness

"It seems like my heart has been battered and bruised so many times that it's developed a real tough skin." Again, passion is a heart issue, not a mental issue. As someone has said, "A good heart is better than all the heads in the world." Yet when our hearts have been crushed and broken, it's hard to revive them with the passion we need for ministry.

In my first year in ministry, a dear older lady taught a kindergarten class down in Room 101. We'll call her Katherine. I don't think Katherine liked me very much. I am sure I made some leadership errors as a youngster just starting out in ministry, but I remember one day in particular when Katherine laid down the law. (I recall thinking on that day, "God loves me, and Katherine has a wonderful plan for my life.")

I had waited until after her kindergarten class to convey some changes we were going to make in children's ministry. As I spoke to her, she simply put her arm around my shoulder and began walking me down the hallway. We got about halfway down the hallway when she said, "Son, let me tell you something about this church. I was here in this church before you came here. I am here now, and I will be here when you have moved on. I just wanted to make sure we were clear today."

Wow! What an energy booster. Talk about excitement for ministry—I could feel the love and joy radiating from the conversation! (Yeah, right.) Actually, I was hurt, battered, and crushed. I began questioning whether I should stay in ministry because I had offended someone. I thought about stopping any changes that I felt we needed, and I didn't sleep well for about a month after this conversation, because I began to worry about what other people thought.

> My first leadership lesson: I am responsible *to* people, not *for* them. And I cannot worry about what others think.

My first leadership lesson: I am responsible *to* people, not *for* them. And I cannot worry about what others think. If you are a leader, then someone is not going to like you. That's just reality. Some people are like a picture window constructed of stained glass. They are either a pane or someone who light shines through.

What can we say to others in these situations, the ones who are already bleeding? If you find yourself relating to this story, then maybe your own heart has developed a few tough calluses. As a result, your passion stays locked inside. Your heart is no longer warm and supple enough to reach out in ministry.

For Reflection and Discussion

1. Does your church tend to have more "workers in the harvest" or more "sleepers in the fields"? Talk about some of the specific reasons for this.

2. Choose the top two "passion poisons" that seem to plague you, your ministry team, or your church in general. What are some practical "antidotes" for you to consider? (If you're studying this book in a group, brainstorm this question for awhile.)

3. Does your ministry team have clearly articulated goals? If not, what plans could you make for a goal-setting process?

4. Have you taken your leaders on an OOTB event? (Suggestion: Take out your calendar right now, and select a date to get OOTB!)

Answers to the Brain Teasers

1. Turn on the first switch, leave it on for ten minutes, and then turn it off. Next, turn on the second switch, and go upstairs to inspect the three bulbs. The hot bulb is controlled by Switch 1; the lit bulb is controlled by Switch 2; and the unlit, cold bulb is controlled by Switch 3.

2. Jackie likes tomatoes. She only likes words that start with prepositions.

3. The wise man tells them to switch camels.

Endnotes

1. The words of Frank Sinatra to his son Frank Sinatra Jr., William Safire and Leonard Safir, *Words of Wisdom* (New York: Simon & Schuster, 1989), 125.

2. Quote from "Vince Lombardi, the Official Website of the Greatest Coach of all time," at http://www.vincelombardi.com/quotes/prepartion.html, accessed September 9, 2001.

3. Quoted in "Developing a Management Vision," Fitness Management at http://www.fitnessworld.com/info_pages/library/mgtmemo/mgtmemo795.html, accessed September 28, 2001.

THREE

→How to Produce Passion

A proud young man of ancient Greece came to Socrates and said, "O great Socrates, I've come to you for knowledge." The venerable philosopher detected some arrogance, so he led the young man through the streets to the sea and put him into the water, chest deep.

"Son, what is it that you want?"

"Knowledge, O wise Socrates!" the young man said with a smile. Socrates put a strong hand on the man's shoulder and thrust him under the water. Thirty seconds later, Socrates let him up and asked, "Son, what is it you want?"

"Wisdom, O great and wise Socrates!" the young man sputtered. Again Socrates pushed the young man under—thirty seconds, thirty-five, then forty seconds passed before he was released. The man was gasping.

"What do you want, young man?"

Between heavy and heaving breaths, the fellow wheezed, "Knowledge, O wise one!"

With that, Socrates jammed him down again—forty seconds...fifty seconds...sixty seconds before the young man was allowed to surface. "What is it that you want?"

"*Air!*" the young man screeched. "I need *air!*"

Then Socrates told him, "When you want knowledge as you have just wanted air, then you will have knowledge."[1]

We need passion as much as we need air; it's obviously not a new concept. When you want something, whether it's for yourself or for others, when you want it the way a drowning man wants air, then you'll have it.

But Craig, you may be thinking, *I'd certainly like to have that kind of passion for my ministry. But I've lost it, and I can't seem to get it back.* You're not alone. Many times in my own life, I've struggled to reignite the spark of passion, and I'm sure you've been there too. If I were a "ministry doctor," I would likely come up with a diagnosis of "myasthenia passionata," that is, "weak passion." If left unattended, the disease gets worse and the prognosis is not good: a steady descent into discouragement and even depression; a loss of energy and love for the work; a tendency toward frustration and conflict with ministry colleagues; and an overall sense of apathy and despair.

If that's you, welcome to my office! The doctor is in, and here is my prescription. Get the passion for ministry back into your soul with these three curative remedies: contagious associations, heartfelt prayer, and daily reminders that mark your defining moments.

Contagious Connections: Getting Close to Passionate People

We've already seen that bad company is deadly. Here's the flip side: If you're not already hanging out with passionate people, then find some, get close, and *catch* their enthusiasm. You'll never hear a passionate person say, "This is good enough." They're always trying to do it a little better because all of their energy and focus is going into the project. One of my college professors used to say, "He who never gets carried away, should be." In other words, every once in a while, it's good to just kind of go over the edge a little bit. Get around people like that.

Along these lines, let's go back and think about Socrates a little more, the man who thought half-drowning a student was good educational practice! We may disagree with his motivational approach, but if we look into his life a bit, we must admit that Socrates was a pretty good example of a passionate person. In the ancient city of Athens (470–399 B.C.), certain philosophers around him, the Sophists, thought it was fun to just sit around and think about things. In contrast, Socrates gave his life, in what he saw as a mission from heaven, to discovering what it really meant to be wise—and getting others engaged in a similar pursuit. Nothing could discourage Socrates from this mission, which he undertook without pay, without starting a school, and without gaining political power or official status. Instead, his method was to walk the streets, talking to the known "experts" and civic leaders in town and simply asking them questions. Under the philosopher's questioning, those who thought themselves wise soon found that most of their beliefs were based on myth, mere convention, or sacred cows that had no rational support.

Few have loved wisdom more passionately than Socrates. He said, "So long as I draw breath and have my faculties, I shall never stop practicing philosophy and exhorting you and elucidating the truth for everyone that I meet."[2] He described his purpose in life as being a stinging fly. His method was to flit around among the "horses" (those who thought they were wise), constantly biting into them with tough questions in hopes of awakening them from their mental slumbers.

(passion)

What's more, he was the ultimate survivor. He lived thorough some of the worst times in Athens, in which for thirty years the Spartans attacked and laid siege to the city. During that time, a terrible plague wiped out a third of the population. The city was eventually conquered, its great navy destroyed, and its proud world dominance reduced to shambles.

But Socrates was still there, walking the streets, spreading the wisdom. He never gave in, even when convicted of treason on a baseless charge (for "corrupting the youth" with unpopular ways of thinking). Sentenced to death, he drank his poison, encouraging the weeping friends at his side to have courage—and to think rationally about the true meaning of life and death.

Why do I tell you about all of this, about things that occurred in Athens centuries ago? To make a surprising point: *Socrates never wrote a single word!* Everything we know about him comes from a man who "hung out" with Socrates, a man named Plato. And without Plato, we would have no Philosophy 101 class over at the junior college! This enthusiastic disciple hung around with a passionate person and shaped the ideas of the Western world for centuries to come.

Of course, our Lord Jesus never wrote anything either. He apparently felt it was better to let his passion flow into those who "hung out" with him, day and night, week after week. That's why he prayed:

> **I have made you [God the Father] known to them [my disciples], and will continue to make you known in order that the love you have for me may be in them and that I myself may be in them.** —John 17:26

> When you find other folks with a burning passion to love and serve this same Savior, stay close to them.

A few short years later, because of the passion that infected Jesus' disciples, the Christians were described as those who had "turned the world upside down." Not bad for a few years' work!

It can be interesting and somewhat enlightening to study a man like Socrates—but it will be thoroughly life changing to study Jesus, to get to know him intimately. After all, he lives and he seeks to reign in your heart at this very moment. Stay close to him; drink in his passion. And when you find other folks with a burning passion to love and serve this same Savior, stay close to them too.

Powerful Prayer: Praying for Passion

The story goes like this: While two pastors' wives sat mending their husbands' pants, one of them said to the other, "My poor Richard is so discouraged. Nothing seems to go right for him at the church, and he's at the point of resigning."

The other replied, "My husband is feeling just the opposite. He's more enthused than ever and senses the Lord's presence in a special way."

A hushed silence fell as they continued to mend the trousers, one patching the seat and the other the knees.[3]

In other words, if you want passion, go to your knees in prayer. James 5:16b reminds us, "The prayer of a righteous man is powerful and effective." So there's really no fancy way of saying it: Stay in a state of prayerful communication with God throughout your day. Yes, we can maintain a spirit of prayer as we go about our tasks. The apostle Paul called it "praying without ceasing" (see I Thessalonians 5:17). How do we do it? It's an attitude!

Martin Luther said, "The fewer the words, the better the prayer."[4] It's not the time you spend doing nothing else but praying; it's the amount of time you spend doing everything else *in a spirit of open dialogue with the Lord*. Communing with God throughout your day will increase your passion for God and his work. How could it be otherwise?

If you want additional intensity in prayer, consider fasting. Take a look at these verses:

> **While they were worshiping the Lord and fasting, the Holy Spirit said, "Set apart for me Barnabas and Saul for the work to which I have called them." So after they had fasted and prayed, they placed their hands on them and sent them off.** —Acts 13:2-3

> **Paul and Barnabas appointed elders for them in each church and, with prayer and fasting, committed them to the Lord in whom they had put their trust.** —Acts 14:23

> If you want passion, you can get it. The question is, Are you willing to pay the price for it?

Fasting really does intensify our prayers. If you want passion, you can get it. The question is, Are you willing to pay the price for it? Are you willing to pray for it? Are you willing to take the next step and sacrifice for it? give up a meal? give up a day of meals, so that you may bring your prayers with intensity before the Lord? As my college baseball coach used to say to me when I was in a hitting slump, "How bad do you want a hit today, Craig?"

"Extremely bad, Coach!" I'd say.

"Then are you willing to do the little things that make the little differences that make the *big* difference?"

In other words, was I willing to pay the price of a little extra practice, a little extra intensity off the field, to win on the field?

Let me make one further point here: We may have gotten into the habit of "hiding" certain parts of our lives from the Lord—the less attractive parts, or the downright ugly parts. If we think of our inner life as the interior of a house with many rooms, we may feel quite comfortable letting the Lord into the "religious" room, or the "competent and disciplined" room, or even the "faithful minister" room. But what about the "sad and angry" room? Can the Lord enter there? Or how about the "lonely" or the "sexually longing" quarters? Are those strictly off-limits? Then there's the big, old basement, the "private sins" area. How could we let Jesus walk down the stairs with us into that terribly messy compartment of our lives?

(passion)

> If we always "clean ourselves up" before approaching the throne of grace, grace never has a chance to do its cleansing work on the parts of us that have grown a bit grimy and tarnished over the years.

Yet he is already there, in every room, inviting you into dialogue about what he knows, asking for your conversation, listening for your pain or discouragement, and yes, as needed, inviting your repentance. If we always "clean ourselves up" before approaching the throne of grace, grace never has a chance to do its cleansing work on the parts of us that have grown a bit grimy and tarnished over the years. Remember: He is the Lord of *all* of you, your whole self. Don't shut him out of the ugly parts, the parts for which he shed his precious blood so long ago.

Finally, I'm sure you've noticed: Sometimes God is silent in response to our requests. Or at least it seems so to us if we're not aware of how God *handles* those requests. First, be assured that God is always present and he's always listening to our heartfelt prayers. And, actually, God does always answer: sometimes "Yes," sometimes "No," and sometimes "Wait." The latter two answers appear as silence to us. But we can come to accept that this is a wise silence. We can realize that our prayers are always *valuable* to God.

Memorable Moments: Keeping Daily Reminders

Along with staying close to passionate people and practicing powerful prayer lives, we can begin to cure our weak passion by keeping a few reminders around us. What do I mean? Let me give you some examples from my own life.

My wife, Mary, has made a scrapbook for each of our boys. In those books, we do more than just collect photographs. We cherish the important moments in our sons' lives. There we find "remember when" from long ago. For instance, on the first page of each book is the little wristband that each child was given when he was born, along with Mary's wristband and my wristband. When we open those pages, we often say, "Remember when…" "Remember when the kids were that small?" "Remember when they checked our wristbands in the newborn nursery?"

Other pages reflect more "interesting" special moments in our kids' lives. Remember when Cameron drew on the hallway walls with a Sharpie pen? Remember when Alec tried to play a peanut-butter-and-marshmallow sandwich in the VCR? I say all of this because these moments are reminders of the investment we've made in our family. This same principle translates to our "ministry family," as well.

With visual reminders around us, we can constantly remember, "Hey, that's what we're all about! That's why we are all here!" We're fired up about it. Our children's ministry has three signs on the wall: One says "Belief." Basically, with God all things are possible. We know it can happen. Another sign says "Grow." Another says "Teamwork." Those are the things we value, and seeing them daily acts as a constant reminder to our staff that this is what we're all about.

> With visual reminders around us, we can constantly remember, "Hey, that's what we're all about! That's why we are all here!"

When I go to speak at children's ministry conferences, I'll often bring with me a little bag of such "reminder goodies" to use as examples. I'll bring a little mug that displays the smiling faces of eight sixth-grade kids on it (along with my not-so-pretty "mug"). On the back it says, "We love you, Craig." Isn't that sweet?

I received that cup from the very first group we started, called "Ten for Ten." Our goal was to gather ten kids and, for ten months, meet with them and teach them some spiritual things, then take them on a mission trip on which they could live out their faith. We put these kids in a van in California and drove all the way to Texas. The mug is now eight years old, but I remember these young women. One of them is now a senior at Baylor University, and the others are also moving ahead to do great things in their lives. The little mug stays on my desk and helps me remember: "Craig, you had something to do with their spiritual growth. That is treasure in heaven." It serves as an empowering moment in my life that keeps me passionate about the present.

One of the other things I bring to show people is a little statue of a wolf—in sheep's clothing. It's precious to me, and here's why: When we wised up and stopped driving to Texas, we started flying. We went from ten to more than thirty sixth-graders on a plane (it's amazing how fast adults will relocate themselves on a plane when you walk onboard with thirty kids). After this particular trip, I was absolutely exhausted.

I remember being on one of the flights home from San Antonio, and it was a quiet time to rest. I felt as if I'd been asleep for an hour, but it was really only a couple of minutes. My wife and I heard our names over the loudspeaker. I looked up and saw five of our kids at the front of the plane making an announcement, and I thought, *What's going on? They've lost it!*

They were thanking me and my wife, presenting us with that little statue. After that, I often taught about a wolf in sheep's clothing, how people sometimes hide their true selves to gain an advantage. I keep the statue on my desk so I can look back at our classes, and the kids we minister to, and think, *This is why we do what we do— because we're making an impact.*

So, what physical reminders could you place around you? What do you need to look at regularly to fire up your passion? to remind you of God's work in your past, his presence within you today, and his plans for your future? Don't ignore this technique because it is a way God has chosen to work with us. In the Old Testament, when the army crossed the Jordan River to conquer the Promised Land, the men set up stones on the far side so all who saw (especially the children) could recall the great things God had done.

> **So Joshua called together the twelve men he had appointed from the Israelites, one from each tribe, and said to them, "Go over before the ark of the Lord your God into the middle of the Jordan.**

Each of you is to take up a stone on his shoulder, according to the number of the tribes of the Israelites, to serve as a sign among you. In the future, when your children ask you, 'What do these stones mean?' tell them that the flow of the Jordan was cut off before the ark of the covenant of the Lord. When it crossed the Jordan, the waters of the Jordan were cut off. These stones are to be a memorial to the people of Israel forever." —Joshua 4:4-7

> Why are physical reminders so powerful? Because *they* *mark our empowering moments.*

Why are physical reminders so powerful? Because *they mark our empowering moments.* In our ministry enrichments at Saddleback, we'll often use a video clip and hand out a little item for reinforcement. For example, we handed out key chains with little metal shoes attached to them. On the shoe is engraved I Corinthians 9:24. As everyone held his or her key chain, we showed a clip from the film *Chariots of Fire.* We used the part where Eric Liddell starts running a race and gets shoved down onto the track. It seems it's over for him—until he gets up and passes one runner after another, eventually winning the race! We then share I Corinthians 9:24: "Do you not know that in a race all the runners run, but only one gets the prize? Run in such a way as to get the prize."

For me, the key chain is a constant reminder of an empowering moment, especially if I have my own fallen-runner-in-the-race experience to tie to it. Most of us do have such times—when we've just wanted to quit, when the work was too overwhelming, when there wasn't enough time and it felt as if we weren't making any headway with our kids or leaders. When I keep my keys on this key chain, every time I start my car, I know that what I'm doing is of great value to the cause of Christ. So mark the moments you've been down and out; mark the times God has lifted you up, dusted you off, and thrust you back in the race. Your passion will bubble up again.

The Key to Passion: *Purpose*

I hope by now you are aware of the power of passion in your life. However, before concluding this chapter, I want to offer a word of caution:

→ Passion does not mean carefree.

→ Passion does not mean careless.

→ Passion does not mean hurry.

→ Passion does not mean busy.

We must organize our lives and ministries to provide the optimum benefits of passion. Before moving offices at our church into our children's ministry area, we had a wall that we called our "ministry wall." It's really a "passion" wall, or a "teamwork" wall. On it, we displayed our mission statement for our children's ministry, which says,

PRACTICAL PATHWAY

Mission and Objectives: Framework for Passion Production

We need to keep clear purposes in mind as a framework within which our passion can work. Usually that calls for slowing down and focusing. The key is to have both dreams and goals, "passion and ration." For most ministries, this will involve two broad steps: (1) creating a *mission statement* and (2) writing *objectives* to carry out that mission in practical ministry.

How do we do it? First, briefly review the STARS mission statement on page 38 as an example. Work with your team to create a statement that defines your own ministry's vision and purpose. Don't rush the process; use as much time as needed to define, as precisely as possible, what you're all about in this ministry. Jot your ideas here, in rough-draft form, to bring to your next team meeting.

Our children's ministry exists to...

_____

_____

The next step after creating your mission statement is to develop objectives in each area of your mission. According to church organizational consultant Robert Worley,[5] each objective written for a ministry (or even for an individual life) should meet as many of the following criteria as possible:

→ **It is goal directed:** It can be clearly seen as a help toward achieving a larger goal.
→ **It is desirable:** It grows out of congregational interests and needs that have been expressed, or represents the leader's conviction about the church's need for a more healthy and effective organization.
→ **It is conceivable:** It can be expressed in clearly understandable words.
→ **It is assignable:** Persons asked to achieve it can clearly see their task.
→ **It is believable:** Its accomplishment can be visualized as entirely possible.
→ **It is achievable:** The existing resources (or those that can be secured) of time, skills, materials, facilities, persons, and dollars are sufficient to do the task.
→ **It is measurable:** It is possible to tell when it has been accomplished and some judgment can be made about whether it was worthwhile to do.
→ **It is controllable:** It produces a minimum of unintended consequences; persons and groups are not involved unintentionally or without their permission.

Now try your hand at writing some objectives related to your mission statement. You may use a format like this for each area:

Mission Area:

_____

Our objectives for the coming week in this area *(list the things you hope to do, and evaluate their priority in light of your mission)*:

_____

_____

_____

_____

_____

Our objectives for the month ahead in this area *(list and prioritize)*:

_____

_____

_____

_____

_____

Our objectives for the next three months in this area *(list and prioritize; think through the steps that need to be planned in advance; begin those processes now)*:

_____

_____

_____

_____

_____

Our objectives for the next year in this area *(list and prioritize; at least every three months, consider whether you're on the right path. Where do you need to make some adjustments?)*:

_____

_____

_____

_____

_____

Our Children's Ministry Exists To
Share Christ with the children of our community, to
Team them with other believers, and to help them
Advance in their spiritual maturity while
Recognizing their spiritual gifts and
Surrendering their lives to God.

So it's share, team, advance, recognize, and surrender—which spells STARS and is why our children's ministry is called "All STARS." That's an example of having a clear purpose. The first step is to develop a mission statement. Then work together to develop your specific objectives.

A sign on a fence in the countryside of Indiana said:

If you cross this field,
You had better do it in 9.8 seconds.
(The bull does it in ten.)

The proposed action would require some planning. Otherwise, a painful disaster could result.

Galatians 4:18a says, "It's fine to be zealous provided the purpose is good." So we want to remember to be passionate all the time, and *for the right purpose.* A certain college basketball coach gained great notoriety for throwing chairs on the basketball court during games when he felt there was a bad call. That's passion—used poorly. You don't want that; you want positive results. Make sure the purpose is right.

> **Never be lacking in zeal, but keep your spiritual fervor, serving the Lord.** —Romans 12:11

That is the right purpose, the right focus.

A recent Christian music video says, "For one small voice, we give our lives." That is so true. One child comes to Christ, one child takes the next step in what it means to grow spiritually, and it's for one small voice that we give our lives. It's for one small voice that we create the energy, the excitement, the enthusiasm, because we've made the difference in the life of a child. That is huge. We don't know what Kingdom difference this one voice will play in history.

So I want you to remember that passion does produce results. When the results are in, they will drive us toward the next step in God's plan for our lives and the church. Remember the great mountain-climbing Sir Hillary? He said,

> **While standing on top of Everest, I looked across the valley, towards the other great peak, Makalu, and mentally worked out a route about how it could be climbed...It wasn't the end of everything for me, by any means. I was still looking beyond to other interesting challenges.**[6]

We are called to climb until we arrive in heaven. In the meantime, our effectiveness here on earth starts with our choice to let God create holy passion within us. Then we can move forward and let it burst out of us and flow into others.

Don't get tired of doing what is good. Don't get discouraged and give up, for we will reap a harvest of blessing at the appropriate time. —Galatians 6:9, NLT

For Reflection and Discussion

1. Do you feel as if you and/or your team have lost some of your passion for ministry? On a scale of 1 to 10, where are you with your passion for children's ministry? List three things you will explore this week to get back your passion.

2. When have you caught someone else's passion? In your group, talk about a person who has most inspired you in your ministry efforts. What can you learn from such folks?

3. Look around your home or office. Do you see any reminders of empowering moments? What will be your first step in getting some empowering moments within your field of vision?

4. From your own study of Scripture, what evidence do you find that Jesus was a passionate person? How did this affect his ministry methods?

5. Who will you breathe passion into this week? Write the name of the person you want to see go to the next level with his or her energy.

6. Brainstorm together: What could we do in our group to make prayer a more central and vital aspect of our fellowship and ministry?

Endnotes

1. Adapted from M. Littleton, Moody Monthly, 1989, p. 24, quoted in "Sermon Illustrations," at http://www.sermonillustrations.com/a-z/w/wisdom.htm, accessed September 2, 2001.

2. Socrates, quoted in David Stewart and H. Gene Blocker, Fundamentals of Philosophy, 2nd ed. (New York: Macmillan, 1987), 16.

3. Illustration adapted from James S. Hewett, ed., Illustrations Unlimited (Wheaton, IL: Tyndale House Publishers, 1988), 356.

4. "Creative Quotations from Martin Luther," at http://www.bemorecreative.com/one/160.htm, accessed September 28, 2001.

5. Adapted from Robert C. Worley, Dry Bones Breathe (Chicago, IL: The Center for the Study of Church Organization Behavior, 1978), 64-65.

6. Edmund Hillary, from the foreword to Peak Performance by Clive Gibson, Mike Pratt, Kevin Roberts and Ed Weymes, as quoted in "Adventurers: Sir Edmund Hillary, King of the World," at www.nzedge.com/heroes/hillary.html, accessed September 2, 2001.

ATTITUDE

"*Whenever trouble comes your way, let it be an opportunity for joy. For when your faith is tested, your endurance has a chance to grow.*"

—James 1:2b-3, NLT

FOUR

→Nose Down, or Nose Up?

It's the most important instrument in the cockpit. As my airline-pilot friend explained, "If you ever get in trouble in an aircraft, the first thing you look at is its attitude."

Not altitude, but attitude—you look at the "attitude" indicator.

"You need to watch your gauges and instruments," he said. "You can't trust your feelings, because they may not be accurate. Especially in darkness, thick fog, or dense clouds, you can't believe what you feel.

I could see the correlations; the analogies were spinning, and we spent the next hour talking about avionics and its similarities to our own struggles with mood and outlook. My friend went on to say that the purpose of the attitude indicator is to tell the pilot whether the plane is basically "nose up" or "nose down." You can imagine how important it is to know that!

And wouldn't it be great if each of us had an internal indicator that would warn us when we were in trouble with our frame of mind? You see, too often we've already crashed—or wrecked someone else—before we notice any indicators of approaching devastation.

> Our *attitude* will determine our *altitude*.

Yet a wise pilot is always monitoring the attitude of the plane, because it indicates the plane's performance. In the interpersonal realm, we might ask ourselves, "In what condition is my attitude at the moment? Is it a nose-up attitude or a nose-down attitude?" That's crucial to know, because our *attitude* will determine our *altitude*.

How high will you go in life? Check your attitude.

What heights will your ministry reach? Check your attitude.

What personal mountaintops will you conquer? Check your attitude.

But sometimes our attitude slips below the horizon. When this happens to me, I have to do a little reflection and quickly consider *why* it's happening.

What Causes That "Attitude Slippage"?

We know that our attitudes don't always stay in good shape. In fact, we all fall into an "I like my bad attitude" day once in a while. Someone has said that having a bad attitude is the art of looking for trouble, finding it everywhere, diagnosing it wrongly, and applying the wrong solutions. That's true. When my attitude begins to slip, it's usually because of one of these bothersome, nose-lowering situations:

→ Turbulence!

Ever had a jolting reminder about why that airplane seat belt is so important? You have, if you've ever dropped through the clouds with an unexpected wind shear. Our self-esteem can take a similar kind of hit and quickly drop to treetop levels. You see, most winds blow horizontally, but under certain atmospheric conditions, a downdraft can suddenly blast straight toward the earth and bring an airplane down several feet. I call it a "whoop de do." Some turbulence is bumpy, some downright scary.

You might experience "self-esteem wind shear" because of a cutting remark at church or a long-term "no-win" situation. Or maybe you have grown up with low self-esteem because of family-of-origin dysfunction, or simply because you long ago fell into a habit of getting down on yourself.

Whatever the cause, wallowing in low-self esteem will ground our attitude and make us ineffective for Christ. I once read about a woman in Florida who died alone at the age of seventy-one. The coroner's report was tragic—"Cause of death: Malnutrition." The dear old lady had wasted away to fifty pounds. Investigators who found her said the place she had lived in was a veritable pigpen, the biggest mess you can imagine. One seasoned inspector declared he'd never seen a residence in greater disarray.

Yet amid the jumble of the unclean, disheveled belongings, investigators found two keys that led them to safe-deposit boxes at two different local banks—which contained close to a million dollars' worth of cash and stock certificates! I heard that the estate would probably fall into the hands of a distant niece and nephew, neither of whom dreamed the lady had a thin dime to her name.

For some reason, this woman must have seen herself as poverty stricken, ignoring the fact of her true wealth. I believe we also sometimes act that way when it comes to our own self-esteem. We are rich in God's favor, yet we deem ourselves unworthy of his love. Christ died to save that "poor" lady. He died to save you. He died to save those kids in your class, too, the ones who like themselves and the ones who don't. Which brings me to two crucial questions:

How do you see yourself? and How does God see you?

Regarding our view of ourselves, it's said that comparison is the root of all inferiority. We find that our low self-esteem is wrapped up in a low self-image in two critical areas illustrated by these questions: (1) Am I lovable? and (2) Am I capable? If you're asking God those questions, the answer is absolutely yes! But sometimes we have a tendency to say, "You know what? No one loves me, and I'm not fit to do the job." But you are fit; God made you fit. We need to see ourselves as God sees us.

How does God see us? Genesis 1:27 says that we were created in God's image, the only beings enjoying that honor. God took the time, effort, and energy to create and fashion us according to his image. First Peter 1:18b-19 says that we were bought with a price, and it was a very expensive price: "It was not with perishable things such as silver or gold that you were redeemed from the empty way of life handed down to you from your forefathers, but with the precious blood of Christ, a lamb without blemish or defect."

How much are you worth? Well, you were worth the death of our Lord, who made himself a sacrificial lamb, just for you!

In light of this incredible truth, is there any reason to compare ourselves with anyone else? After all, we can always find someone who's doing it better than we are—or worse than we are. So what's the point? Let's look through God's eyes and consider, "How does he see me?"

If we forget to view our worth, our eternal value, as God sees it, our attitudes can begin to slip into the "nose-down" position.

→Locking Up!

Whatever happens, when you're flying a plane, don't panic! The passengers are depending on you to keep a level head. It's certainly possible to experience serious failures while in flight, but locking up never helps. Some of us are so afraid to fail that we never even get into the cockpit.

Yes, fear of failure can be devastating. This sad fact reminds me of another interesting instrument on the newer airplanes, something that caught my attention as I talked with my pilot friend. It's called the "flight director." This instrument gives the pilot specific commands to follow while in flight—what air speed to maintain, when to decrease pitch, when to turn, when to accelerate. And it's tied into the total navigation system. The flight director tells pilots what they need to be doing.

It's great that God didn't create us as robots, but gave us his Word. The flight director tells the plane how to fly in all situations, just as God's Word can guide us through our days, in all situations. It tells us when to speed up, when to slow down, when to turn. And it gives us a constant readout of our attitude and altitude in life. In other words, it keeps our lives "flying high."

Along with going to the Word when we're caught up in the fear of failure, one of the best things we can do is to sit calmly and contemplate this question: *What is the worst that could happen if I fail?* We should name the *specific* consequences of a potential failure—and not let our imagination make it any bigger than it will likely be. "Concretizing" our fears keeps our imagination on the sidelines, not allowing what psychologists call "awfulizing" to blow things out of proportion. Usually, the imagined consequences are far worse than the actual potential harm that would spring from our failures.

I heard someone say, "People who don't see themselves winning are often obsessed with losing." I know sometimes we're afraid to fail. But sometimes we have to crawl out on the edge of the limb, because that's where the fruit is.

→Flaming Out!

We all seem to live with a constant "need for speed." But living on pure adrenaline, rushing and straining, will soon send our attitude into a tailspin and completely burn us out.

I asked my pilot friend, "Can you fly a big airliner on one engine?"

"Yes, it's part of the safety regulations to be able to fly the aircraft on one engine," he said. "So when both engines are running, they're normally operating at about 60 percent capacity."

This is the final takeaway for all of us who must have complete control, who always work until it gets done, who push, push, push (in other words, the workaholics out there—you know who you are): You may be using too much energy. Your attitude and performance could actually improve *if you just reduced your speed!*

It's no use for you to get up early and stay up late, working for a living. The Lord gives sleep to those he loves. —Psalm 127:2, NCV

Honestly, the most Christlike thing some of us can do today is sleep in. Maybe rent a movie and pop a bag of popcorn—renew, refresh, rejuvenate. I would say that the times in my life when my attitude is the worst is when I am moving too fast. When I'm rushing around and playing "top gun" in this dogfight of ministry, I don't actually see the people in front of me.

> The times in my life when my attitude is the worst is when I am moving too fast.

I've not only observed it in myself, but I've seen it in my staff. The great folks on my staff are the "flamers." They are the choleric, lionhearted personalities most prone to burn out. They get caught up in getting it done; however, when it *doesn't* get done, they're likely to do it themselves (and then become angry with the person they've partnered with—and there goes the attitude). Recognize anyone here?

I recognize myself—an overworked person sporting a less-than-attractive attitude. We must remember to *slow down*. Ask yourself and the people around you, "When is the last time you were on vacation—without your palm pilot?"

→Circling, Circling, Circling...

It's the classic, urgent, frequent-flier query: "So why haven't we landed *yet?*" Stranded far above Runway 9—and going nowhere—you know how frustrating it can be to have to live with your unmet expectations. Life's minor expectations are the little attitude destroyers. But suppose you're expecting something big, expecting God to give you a happy, successful life, for instance?

But is that what God promised? Didn't Jesus say, "In the world you'll have a lot of trouble"? As author Scott Peck said in the first sentence of his book *The Road Less Traveled*: "Life is difficult."[1] If we refuse to accept that most basic, all-encompassing truth about existence, our attitudes will nose-dive.

(attitude)

Here is what I know: You will never be an effective leader without experiencing some type of pain or difficulty in your life. Thirteen years ago, I would not have said this. But after talking to others in ministry and observing it firsthand myself, I detect one commonality in all effective leaders: They have faced difficulty, discouragement, and disappointment.

James said,

> **Dear brothers and sisters, whenever trouble comes your way, let it be an opportunity for joy. For when your faith is tested, your endurance has a chance to grow. So let it grow, for when your endurance is fully developed, you will be strong in character and ready for anything.** —James I:2-4, NLT

You see, it says *whenever*—not *if*—trouble comes your way, everything from circling with unmet expectations to crashing in pain. God uses these things to conform us to his image. I am reminded of this pain each time I visit my son Blake's grave (who was stillborn). The words from 2 Corinthians 12:9 (GWT) are written on his gravestone: "But he told me: 'My kindness is all you need. My power is strongest when you are weak.' So I will brag even more about my weaknesses in order that Christ's power will live in me."

We need to keep a clear perspective on life and a clear perspective on our expectations. For example, have you ever been in a hurry and hit every red light on the way to your destination? Your attitude degraded, block by block, right? But suppose you had *expected* every light to be red? Then whenever you hit a green light, you would have been fired up, excited that you had hit a green one. The trouble with circling is our *expectations*. If we change our expectations—I said change, not lower—we will provide some needed room for our attitudes to flourish.

→Bad Weather!

What do you do when someone blows a little hot air your way? or you experience a major lightning strike? or perhaps someone rains on your parade? How's your attitude in these situations?

When conflict goes unresolved, our attitudes head straight downhill. There also are warning indicators in an airplane's cockpit to let the pilot know how the engine is performing. One of them is the engine oil indicator. Now the purpose of the oil, of course, is to decrease friction so that all the parts of the engine can work in harmony.

Because we work to equip and empower people, the goal is to function like a friction-free jet engine. All parts are designed to do specific tasks, all working in concert to perform for the Lord. Our attitudes—the interpersonal "oil"—are the friction reducer. But if the oil hasn't been changed regularly, or the viscosity has broken down, the engine ceases to function. Have you ever thought of it this way? Here are some ways your attitude is like oil:

→You have to continually check it.

→It reduces friction in your life.

→It needs to be changed regularly.

How to Adjust That Attitude!

Are there any immediate corrective actions you can take to "bring your nose up" as you fly through life and ministry? Yes! Here's something, having to do with Scripture memorization, that's worked for me:

When I was in college, I began copying verses that would really strike me and powerfully influence my spiritual growth. I called them the "Why Should I's?" I gathered about a hundred of these verses, and they've helped me immensely ever since. Below are my top seven. To make them practical and relevant for you, think through each one in terms of issues and concerns you face in your daily life. You may wish to journal some of your thoughts in the spaces provided.

1. Why should I lack strength—when those who hope in the Lord will find spiritual renewal and great energy for his work (Isaiah 40:31)?

   The times I feel the most "wiped out" and exhausted in ministry are when...

   _____

   _____

   _____

2. Why should I be afraid—when I believe that God didn't give me a spirit of fear, but of power, love, and self-control (2 Timothy 1:7)?

   My greatest fear at the moment is...

   _____

   _____

   _____

3. Why should I lack wisdom—when the Bible says that if I need wisdom, I should just ask God for it because he gives generously (James 1:5)?

   Lord, I need your wise guidance for...

   _____

   _____

   _____

4. Why should I be worried—when the Bible says to cast all my anxiety on him, because he cares for me (1 Peter 5:7)?

Help! I'm really worried about...

_____

_____

_____

5. Why should I feel all alone—when Jesus says he'll be with me always, even until the end of the age (Matthew 28:20)?

I know you're here, Jesus, but I feel the loneliest when...

_____

_____

_____

6. Why should I let the pressures of everyday life get to me—when Jesus, who overcomes the world, promises me peace (John 16:33)?

I'm mostly pressured these days by...

_____

_____

_____

7. Why should I be concerned about the days ahead—when the Bible says the Lord has great plans for my future (Jeremiah 29:11)?

My concerns about the future revolve around...

_____

_____

_____

Additional Suggestion for Personal Application: Meditate on the seven Scripture verses above. Then take these steps:

→ Jot your favorite verses on note cards, and keep them in your wallet or purse. Work on memorizing them whenever you have a spare moment during the day.

→ Explore the context of these verses. Go back and read the Bible chapters in which these verses are found, focusing on one chapter per week during your time of study.

→ Go back and read the entire Bible book for each verse, staying in one book per month.

→ Work on creating a second "top seven" for yourself, as new issues and concerns surface in your life.

→ Enjoy your renewed attitude—and your higher altitude!

→ Without it you will freeze up and break.

→ If there are impurities in it, it is useless.

→ If it leaks, people know it.

→ If it's clean, it produces a long-lasting engine.

We'll go into depth about conflict resolution in Chapter 11, but let me say here that if family members have unresolved conflict at home, it will filter into every other area of their lives. When children come to church on Sunday morning, they bring with them what they've experienced at home throughout the week. I know sometimes we have a tendency to look at those kids and say, "Oh boy, what an *opportunity* this week! After this tough week, I believe God is calling me to the singles ministry."

Those kids need you, with the right attitude, because you may be the only Jesus they see that week. We've got to make sure our attitudes are right to lead those kids to the next level and maybe introduce them, for the first time, to a personal relationship with the God who made them.

Sure, bad weather will come; it's guaranteed. But as we fly through those times of *opportunity*, let's keep a close eye on our oil indicators so we can function friction-free with our attitudes.

> We've got to make sure our attitudes are right to lead those kids to the next level and maybe introduce them, for the first time, to a personal relationship with the God who made them.

Ready to "Fly High" in Ministry?

Consider the basic nature of flight: The speed of the air over the wing is faster than the speed of the air under the wing. This creates more pressure under the wing to push it up for flight. The flaps on the wing move so that the shape of the wing can change, which is critical to generating lift at a slower speed.

I have been serving in children's ministry for thirteen years. During that time, I've often wanted to call it quits and cash it in—buy a Walkman and wash windows in solitude until Jesus comes back. There have been times the pressure flowing *over* my wings was so intense that I did not want to fly. In fact, I couldn't fly! My attitude aerodynamics just weren't right.

But I've found that when those times hit, I wasn't watching my attitude in the least, focusing only on surviving. Can you imagine what would happen if a pilot flew while looking out of only the side windows?

The same is true with our attitudes. We must refuse to focus on the circumstances around us. Here's what I know: Things may be going great, everything is rolling along, and what happens next is that you will get cocky or arrogant. Your EGO

(attitude)

will soar (EGO = Edging God Out), and you'll be on your way—to a bad attitude. Or things may go downhill so fast that your head spins. For example, all the volunteers have just resigned, you are discouraged with your current ministry because you just went to a conference and came away with one idea and a boatload of depression, and everyone else "appears" to have their act together.

In either case, a focus on circumstances alone is deadly to your good attitude. Focus instead on Christ. Have this attitude in yourselves, which was also in Christ Jesus:

Who, being in very nature God, did not consider equality with God something to be grasped, but made himself nothing, taking the very nature of a servant, being made in human likeness.

And being found in appearance as a man, he humbled himself and became obedient to death—even death on a cross!

Therefore God exalted him to the highest place and gave him the name that is above every name, that at the name of Jesus every knee should bow, in heaven and on earth and under the earth, and every tongue confess that Jesus Christ is Lord, to the glory of God the Father.

Therefore, my dear friends, as you have always obeyed—not only in my presence, but now much more in my absence—continue to work out your salvation with fear and trembling, for it is God who works in you to will and to act according to his good purpose.

Do everything without complaining. —Philippians 2:7-14

Adjust your flaps. As if flying, use the pressure of the wind above and below your wings to generate lift. This week, this month, this year, respond when you feel your attitude slipping by

1. **Looking Up:** Keep your focus on what God is doing in the kingdom. "Set your minds on things above, not on earthly things…Your life is now hidden with Christ in God" (Colossians 3:2-3).

2. **Slowing Down:** We all make better choices when we pause a moment.

3. **Reaching Out:** Focus on helping others reach their potential.

These three responses can help keep you on the right flight path with your attitude. When you look up, slow down, and reach out to others, the lives of your kids and the lives of your adult team members will be encouraged and renewed—just because they've come into contact with a flier with the proper attitude.

For Reflection and Discussion

(attitude)

1. How would you describe your typical attitude as you wake up each morning? (If your team has reached the maturity level to do so comfortably, allow time for the group to give feedback on the attitude "strengths and weaknesses" of each individual. Focus on the positive!)

2. When has your self-esteem taken a sudden hit? How did you cope? What insights can you share related to doing ministry during those times?

3. Is there anyone in your life who seems to cause your attitude to slip? Write that person's name and begin to pray for him or her this week.

4. Which nose-lowering situation seems to plague you (or your group) the most? Talk about some practical solutions!

5. Have you ever felt like quitting? Write five reasons you will not give up working with kids—and then put your words in a safe place, where you can find them next week.

6. Finish the following sentences:

   This week I will look up by...

   This week I will slow down by...

   This week I will reach out by...

Endnote

1. M. Scott Peck, M.D., *The Road Less Traveled: A New Psychology of Love, Traditional Values and Spiritual Growth* (New York: Simon & Schuster, 1978), 1.

FIVE

→Shake It Off...and Step Up!

The mule fell into the farmer's well. Hearing the old mule braying, and after carefully considering the situation, the farmer decided that neither the mule nor the well were worth saving. So he called his neighbors from around town and enlisted them to haul some dirt with him. The plan was to fill up the well, burying the mule in the process.

As soon as the dirt came cascading down the well, the old mule became hysterical. It brayed and it kicked.

The dirt kept coming, more and more falling onto that poor mule's back—until suddenly it dawned on the animal that it could just shake it off and then step up onto the growing pile.

So that's what it did. The mule shook it off and stepped up, shook it off and stepped up. It repeatedly encouraged itself by making a choice (to the extent a mule can make a choice) by shaking it off and stepping up.

No matter how painful the blows or how distressing the situation seemed, the old mule fought the panic of the situation and just kept shaking it off and stepping up. It wasn't long before the old mule, battered and exhausted, stepped triumphantly over the wall of the well. What seemed like it would bury the mule, actually ended up blessing it and became the way out—all because of the attitude with which the mule handled the situation.

We've all been in the dry well at times, and we've all felt the dirt crashing down on our backs. At those times, we face a stark choice: Shake it off and step up or lie down and get buried.

It's Your Choice!

Yes, our attitude is always a matter of choice. But let's think a little deeper about this. The key to choosing the most helpful and productive attitude is being able to distinguish between response and reaction.

Not too long ago, I found my way to my doctor's office for some medication. My doctor wrote a prescription, and I began to take the pills. Let's just say they didn't help; in fact, the medicine he originally gave me caused other problems. He said I was having a negative reaction to the medication, so he wrote a new prescription. After a few days on the new medicine, I responded well and didn't need to go back.

> *The attitude you use is the attitude you choose.* No one else chooses it for you—not your boss, not your mom, not your friends, not your spouse. You choose it.

Our attitudes are a bit like medication. We either *respond* well or *react* negatively to our circumstances. We don't want to react. If you take some medication and begin feeling better, you're *responding* to the medication. That is, you are reducing the symptoms—and probably attacking the cause—of the original problem. So we need to respond correctly to our circumstances, and unlike when taking medication, that is purely our choice.

The attitude you use is the attitude you choose. No one else chooses it for you—not your boss, not your mom, not your friends, not your spouse. You choose it.

It's true. The way you think about a situation before you enter it will greatly affect its outcome. So if you're coming in Sunday morning with a rotten attitude, it's going to be a tough morning. Now, I've got to be honest with you. Sometimes I show up on the weekend and I'm tired. Maybe I've had a flat tire on the way, or maybe I just don't want to be in church at all that day. But, sadly, I will bring this attitude of frustration to the kids I minister to, no matter what age they are. I have to continually remind myself: The way I'm thinking *before* I enter the church today will greatly affect the outcome of my leadership efforts *during* my time with those kids and leaders.

There's solid biblical support for what I'm saying here. Consider the experience of Paul and Silas in Acts 16. These two missionary buddies were in the city of Philippi when a slave girl began following them around, shouting: "These men are servants of the Most High God, who are telling you the way to be saved."

Now this normally laudable verbal outpouring wasn't because of her intense devotion to the Lord Almighty. No, she'd been making lots of money for her handlers by predicting the future in sideshows along the city streets. It seems she had a spirit dwelling in her that gave her occult powers. So she knew who the missionaries were, and she was becoming a real pain.

Anyway, when the owners of this girl watched Paul cast out her demon—and throw away their chances for making more big bucks—they brought the preachers to the authorities, and complained, "These men are Jews, and are throwing our city into an uproar by advocating customs unlawful for us Romans to accept or practice."

(attitude)

Paul and Silas were going to have a bad day. A public beating followed, with the crowds joining in the attack against them. The Roman officers tore the clothes off Paul and Silas and beat them. Then the men were thrown into prison. The jailer was ordered to guard them carefully. When he heard this order, the jailer put them far inside the jail, not just on one of those fringe cells—we're talking *deep*. He even pinned down their feet with large chunks of wood.

So what did Paul and Silas choose to do at this point? Consider:

→ *Did they moan and cry?*

→ *Did they complain and argue?*

→ *Did they call their lawyers and start planning a suit?*

→ *Did they question the goodness of God?*

→ *Did they become confused and depressed about the role of suffering in the world?*

→ *Did they get crabby and confrontational—or sullen and withdrawn?*

All of these things would have been legitimate options. Any of them would have been tempting for any of us. But what did the two bruised and bleeding men choose to do?

They decided to pray and sing hymns.

Pray. Sing.

Sing?

Sometimes when someone cuts in front of me on the freeway, I can develop a bad attitude in less than two seconds. And the trouble is that, as a Christian, I don't have enough gestures to use at a time like that. Well, here are Paul and Silas, who did nothing wrong. They felt the stinging thud of leather upon their backs, leather knotted with sharp bits of metal or bone so it was sure to cut the flesh. They endured the taunts of an ugly crowd while bleeding into the dirt. Their captors stuck their hands and feet into sharp-edged shackles.

They chose to sing.

Suddenly, a strong earthquake shook the foundation of the prison. All the cell doors rattled open, and all the prisoners walked out into the hallway. The jailer woke up and saw that the doors were open and, thinking that everybody had escaped, he got out a sword and was about to put himself to death (which was the punishment for an incompetent guard in that day).

But if you look at verse 28, you'll see that Paul shouted, "Don't harm yourself! We are all here!" Now, I don't know about you, but if I were Paul, I would have been thinking, *I've been beaten, I've been whipped. If an earthquake has opened the doors, I'm going to get out of here.* I would have believed that was God's call to leave!

But Paul and Silas didn't do that. They chose to stay.

The guard brought them outside and said, "Sirs, what must I do to be saved?" And Paul and Silas led him to Christ, along with his entire family.

What an amazing conclusion to a story that started out with a bad day getting worse! But it all hinged on a choice of attitude—not the circumstances, the attitude.

Attitude "Interprets" Your World

In one of my favorite movies, *Father of the Bride II*, there's a great sequence where George (played by Steve Martin) and his wife, Nina (played by Diane Keaton), have just found out they are pregnant at an "older" age. They are driving down the street, and Nina is looking out the window, seeing cute little girls in her mind's eye. The little girls are all dressed up, skipping through town in slow motion, the epitome of blessed childhood innocence. George, on the other hand, is looking out his window and seeing screaming, out-of-control, obnoxious little children whining their way to their wants.

> The way we think about a situation before we enter it greatly affects its "reality" for us. In a sense, our judgments about anything will determine what it is for us. Our interpretations, to a large extent, become our world.

Here is the point: The way we think about a situation before we enter it greatly affects its "reality" for us. In a sense, our judgments about anything will determine what it is for us. Our interpretations, to a large extent, become our world.

Do you agree?

I'm simply saying that all the aspects of your reality, day by day, are not given to you. Yes, some parts are given. But your interpretations of a situation add to the "givens" and slant it one way or another. The slant can be toward the negative and discouraging. On the other hand, you can slant things toward the positive and hopeful. You see, other people don't *create* your spirit, they only *reveal* it. In other words,

Today I can complain because the weather is rainy, or I can be thankful that the grass is getting watered for free.

Today I can cry because roses have thorns, or I can celebrate that thorns have roses.

Today I can mourn my lack of friends, or I can excitedly embark upon a quest to discover new relationships.

Today I can whine because I have to go to work, or I can shout for joy that I have a job to do.

Today I can complain that I have to go to school, or I can open my mind and fill it with rich new tidbits of knowledge.

Today I can murmur because I have to clean the house, or I can feel honored that the Lord has provided shelter for me.

The great thing is that you can make the choice on how to live this day. Someone may cut you off on the freeway, and that's not your choice. How you respond to it *is*. Someone may not like the new program you are starting at your church for the children. That's their choice. How you respond to them is your choice. Your budget may have been reduced (maybe you're saying, "What's a budget?"). That is the board's choice. How you respond to the decision is your choice. Is this great or what! We get

(attitude)

to choose what type of day we're going to have! Pastor and author Chuck Swindoll said it like this:

> **The longer I live, the more I realize the impact of attitude on life. Attitude is more than facts; it's more important than the past, than education, than money, than circumstances and failures, than successes, than what other people think or say or do. It is more important than appearance, giftedness or skill. It will make or break a company, it will cause a church to soar or sink. It will be the difference between a happy home and a home of horror. It's attitude, and the remarkable thing is, you have a choice every day regarding the attitude you will embrace for that day. We cannot change our past, we cannot change the tick of the clock and we cannot change the march towards death. We cannot change the fact that people will act in a certain way. We cannot change the inevitables. I am convinced that life is 10 percent what happens to me, and 90 percent how I respond to it.**[1]

OK, so you're convinced that attitude is your choice. And you realize it's an important choice because your attitude will actually interpret your world for you. So now you're ready to raise the question that logically follows: What actions can help me develop and maintain a *sanctified* attitude? The following "sanctifiers" will help you respond in obedience to the Scripture that says,

> **Your attitude should be the same as that of Christ Jesus.**
> —Philippians 2:5

→Sanctifier I: Start a Habit of Seeking the Joy

The more we repeat an action, the more habitual it becomes. An action repeated becomes an attitude realized. In other words, we can make habits out of anything: eating chocolate-covered donuts on the way home from work every evening or lifting our hearts to God's presence as we arise every morning.

The apostle Paul said in Philippians 4:4, "Rejoice in the Lord always. I will say it again: Rejoice!" That is the habit we want, the habit of seeking out the joy in every situation—not that the *circumstances* will always be happy. Far from it! In fact, consider the historical situation when Paul wrote those words. Was this written in a time when things were easy? No, this was the era of Emperor Nero, one of the most evil rulers in history. Just consider a portion of his biography:

→He was born to a mother (Agrippina) who had poisoned her previous husband—and then poisoned Nero's father.

→He killed his wife, Octavia, so he could marry his mistress, Poppaea.

→He killed Poppaea because she complained that he came home late.

→He was the likely motivator behind two devastating fires in Rome, although he blamed them on the Christians.

→ He killed Christians in the most horrendous ways, sometimes burning them as "torches" to light the palace grounds.

→ He dressed up in disguises at night and attacked people on the street. If they fought back, he killed them and threw their bodies in the sewers.

→ He reinstated the Olympic Games in Rome and "won" six gold medals—without finishing even one event!

→ He eventually committed suicide.

What a grotesque résumé! My point is that Paul and Silas certainly couldn't make circumstances their source of rejoicing. Their whole society was in a mess! No, they would rejoice *in the Lord*.

→ Sanctifier 2: Surrender the Moment

"Your attitude should be the same that Christ Jesus had" (Philippians 2:5, NLT). There are two particular times this verse must kick into high gear for you: (1) when things don't go as planned, and (2) when you feel you're being treated unfairly.

So often things don't go our way. For example, have you ever had a bur in your sock? Think about that. Suppose you've been walking along in the woods, following a trail along a beautiful mountain vista, and you picked up a few of those nasty, sticky, prickly things that end up in your socks. Suppose further that they began to prick at your ankles and bite into the skin on your shins. You have to stop, sit on a rock, and start picking those rotten little barbs out of your socks and pant legs. You hate the little burs, you hate the aggravation, and you hate wasting hiking time on getting rid of those burs!

If you're like most of us, the irritation would give rise to a bad attitude.

But if you happened to be a man named George de Mestral, and those were your socks on a lovely summer day in the Swiss Alps in 1948, you would have seen things a little differently. As George peeled burs from his socks, he began to think of these bothersome sticklers as "nature's little fasteners." Would you have thought of them like that?

When George got home that day, he decided to take a look at the little burs under his microscope. He was amazed and inspired. "What a wonderful latching system—all those tiny hooks!" he thought. Being an amateur inventor, he thought, "Maybe I could design something like this that people could use to keep things closed—and open easily, too."

Do you know what he eventually came up with? It was a wonderful invention called by a name that combines the words "velour" and "crochet"—*Velcro*.

That's right. George de Mestral turned his frustration with itchy, scratchy pant legs into an incredible product. Earning a patent in 1955, Velcro Industries was soon selling over 60 million yards of his synthetic thorns per year. We, too, can take the "burs" of life and turn them into something useful—by surrendering our moments to creativity and the Holy Spirit's leading.

The second kind of situation—when we most need to have the mind of Christ—is when we're treated unfairly. Chuck Swindoll talks about the effects of helplessness, cited in New York magazine. The story dealt with the example of Maj. F. J. Harold Kushner, an army medical officer held by the Viet Cong for almost six years. Among the prisoners in Kushner's POW camp was a tough young marine, twenty-four-years-old, who had already survived two years of prison-camp life in relatively good health. Part of the reason for this was that the camp commander had promised to release the man if he cooperated. Because this had been done before with others, the marine turned into a model POW and the leader of the camp's "thought-reform group." As time passed, he gradually realized that his captors had lied to him. When the full truth hit him, he went into a psychological shock, becoming, in effect, a zombie. He walked around in a stupor, refused to do all work, rejected all offers of food and encouragement. Most of the time, he simply lay on his cot sucking his thumb. And within a matter of weeks, he was dead.[2]

Dr. Martin Segglemen of the University of Pennsylvania attributes the marine's death to the attitude of helplessness. That is a way we can choose to react in the face of extreme disappointment, when we've been severely cheated out of our hopes and dreams. But we can also choose to surrender those hopes, too, just as Jesus did:

Who, being in very nature God, did not consider equality with God something to be grasped. —Philippians 2:6

The beauty of surrender is that, whatever it is we are holding on to so tightly, whatever seems to be saving us from despair, is usually the thing that is keeping us from intimate fellowship with our Lord. When we let go, our hands and hearts are free to embrace him fully. What could be better than that?

→Sanctifier 3: Serve the Body

A story of unknown source, which is circulating on the Internet, speaks of a penetrating picture of sacrificial serving. Whether it actually happened or not, it provides a powerful example for us. As the account goes, after a forest fire in the mountains of America's West, park rangers began a trek up the slopes to assess the inferno's damage. One ranger found a bird literally petrified in ashes, perched statuesquely on the ground at the base of the tree. Somewhat sickened by the eerie sight, he knocked over the bird with a stick.

According to various accounts, when he struck the bird, three tiny chicks scurried out from under their dead mother's wings. The loving mother bird, apparently aware of impending disaster, had carried her offspring to the base of the tree and had gathered them under her wings. Somehow she must have known that the toxic smoke would rise. She could have flown to safety but had refused to abandon her babies. As the blaze arrived and the heat singed her own body, the mother remained steadfast. Because she'd been willing to die, those under the cover of her wings would live.

The Bible says,

If you serve Christ with this attitude, you will please God. And other people will approve of you, too. So then, let us aim for harmony in the church and try to build each other up. —Romans 14:18-19, NLT

Do You Know the ABCs of Attitude Adjustment?

How will you react the next time you need to "shake it off and step up"? Let me offer a suggestion:

In the 1950s, psychologist Albert Ellis developed a system of counseling called "rational emotive behavioral therapy."[3] He used the letters ABCDE to explain how our interpretations of events in our lives, our *attitudes*, can radically affect our emotions (our happiness and peace):

Activating experience: Something occurs.

Belief system: I *interpret* the event according to my beliefs.

Consequent emotions: My interpretative "self-talk" causes feelings.

In this system, events aren't causing the feelings; rather, our interpretations of these events are the immediate cause of any fear, anger, sadness, or other so-called negative emotions. For example,

Activating Experience/Event: A man walks up to you on the street, with a grimacing scowl on his face, tightly gripping a baseball bat.

Belief/Self-talk: I am about to be mugged—and beaten to a pulp!

Consequent Emotions: You experience intense fear and anxiety.

Note that the *event* did not cause your feelings. You have *interpreted* the situation as one of great danger. But suppose the man said, "I was just robbed by a guy with a baseball bat. I grabbed the bat from him—but not before he hit me. Can you help me, please?"

Clearly, events themselves do not always cause our emotions, because there is not always a direct connection between A and C. But events *do* start our thinking, or "self-talk," about what we believe is happening (B). That's when we need to counter any wrong assumptions. This leads to the next two steps in Ellis' system:

Dispute irrational beliefs: Replace any misguided or false beliefs with the truth.

Eliminate the misperception: Feel the *appropriate* emotion.

Ellis was a humanist psychologist; however, all truth is God's truth, and the Bible calls for a similar approach in attacking our false belief systems when our attitude does a nose dive. Consider this Scripture:

> **Brothers, whatever is true, whatever is noble, whatever is right, whatever is pure, whatever is lovely, whatever is admirable—if anything is excellent or praiseworthy—think about such things.** —Philippians 4:8

Suggestion for Practical Application: Think back to the last emotion-churning situation that came your way. Maybe your ministry leader or pastor called to ask you why a certain event didn't go as planned, or maybe you faced harsh criticism about one of your programming ideas. Take some time to place yourself back in the scene, and recall the thoughts that quickly bubbled up in your mind. Jot some responses:

1. **Recall:** What "automatic" thoughts/beliefs surfaced immediately?

   (For example: "Oh no! My pastor surely thinks I'm a complete idiot. He doesn't like what I did; he must not like me, either!")

   _____

   _____

   _____

   _____

   _____

   _____

2. **Reconsider:** Challenge those beliefs for a moment, by asking yourself,

   → Is there any evidence *for* this belief?
   → What is the evidence *against* this belief?
   → What is the worst that can happen if I give up this belief?
   → What is the best that can happen?

3. **Record:** Write it ASAP. For the future, make a habit of writing your automatic thoughts and beliefs as soon as you can after a potentially attitude-blowing event. Then open yourself to alternative interpretations (why not pray and ask God to guide you here?). As you regularly practice these steps, you can expect your automatic thoughts and interpretations to gradually move more into line with Philippians 4:8.

> It takes sacrifice
> and loving
> service to "build
> one another up."

It takes sacrifice and loving service to "build one another up." It is virtually an act of protection for those we love: When we build one another up, we give one another the resources to defend ourselves from doctrinal error, from family dysfunction, from moral decay. In giving ourselves in this way, however, we make a life-saving difference to children and families. Sometimes we can feel the flames licking our heels. But we must simply put up our wings and serve the body by serving our kids—yes, even when we feel like stopping because the joy is gone and, yes, even when we feel as if our work is more like a "job" than a "ministry."

Of course, we're not called to be doormats; sometimes we have to take intentional and firm action as a means of serving. In *Before You Quit*, Blaine Allen tells a story of taking just that kind of action.

A principal at a small middle school faced an unusual problem: Girls would apply lipstick in the bathroom, and then press their lips to the mirror.

The result? Lip prints.

Fun!

But not fun for the school custodian.

Before the problem got out of hand, the principal gathered the young women and took them to the women's room to meet with him and the school custodian. The principal explained that every night the janitor found it increasingly difficult to clean the mirror.

"I don't believe you ladies understand what a problem it is for Mr. Jones to wash these mirrors, so I've asked him to show us what it takes."

The custodian took a long-handled brush out of a box, dipped it into the nearest *toilet*, walked to the mirror, and scrubbed clean the lipstick. That was the last day the girls pressed their lips to the mirror![4]

Whether in a small-town school or a ministry, leadership often means headaches. People don't always do what they should. Whether intentional or unintentional, through ignorance or immaturity, people make messes. And guess who has to keep the mirrors clean?

So we take sacrificial action—whether through compassionate service or the service of tough love (which is also compassionate). Legitimate concerns always demand a response. Serving the body well often means that leadership must act before things get out of hand.

→Sanctifier 4: Support the Team

The apostle Paul uttered this blessing upon the Roman Christians:

> **May God, who gives this patience and encouragement, help you live in complete harmony with each other—each with the attitude of Christ Jesus toward the other.** —Romans 15:5, NLT

According to Thomas Leppert, chairman and CEO of the Turner Corporation in Dallas, "A successful team boils down to two things: mutual respect among team

(attitude)

members and a common vision about where the team is going." We're going to talk more about team success in Chapter 9, but for now I'll simply raise this question: *Does your team know where it's going—and can you all get excited about it together?*

Remember that the church at Philippi was struggling with division. Paul starts Philippians 2 with four questions:

→ *Does your life in Christ give you strength?*

→ *Does his love comfort you?*

→ *Do we share together in the spirit?*

→ *Do you have mercy and kindness?*

I can't add much to that, an excellent evaluation tool for any team. I suggest that you spend time in a future team meeting just raising the questions. The attitude of each team member will make all the difference in how those questions are ultimately answered.

In fact, your attitude is the major determining factor between success and failure. Top executives know this. Here is how they hire personnel (this is from the largest salaried executives in the United States):

→5 percent—availability

→5 percent—adaptability

→10 percent—ability

→10 percent—appearance

→70 percent—attitude[5]

An attitude of support and encouragement is invaluable in any team member, whether in business or in the church. Such an attitude truly shines (1) when you don't always agree with everyone on the team, and (2) when you don't yet know the direction the team is going. Can you be that kind of team member?

When All Is Lost—Is It?

Victor Frankl was a Jewish psychiatrist taken to the Nazi concentration camps during World War II. They took virtually everything from him. They killed his father, mother, brother, and wife. The Nazis took all his possessions, took his wedding ring, took his clothes, and even shaved his head.

Frankl said, "While we were waiting for the shower, our nakedness was brought home to us: we really had nothing now except our bare bodies—even minus hair; all we possessed, literally, was our naked existence."[6]

But as Frankl stood before the German commandant, it dawned upon him that there would always be one thing they could never take from him: his choice of attitude. In fact, after the war he even developed an entire system of psychology (called logotherapy) based upon this insight: that when we are reduced to our most basic essence, the thing that remains is our ability to decide how we will respond.

The experiences of camp life show that man does have a choice of action. There were enough examples, often of a heroic nature. Frankl continues, "We who lived in concentration camps can remember the men who walked through the huts comforting others, giving away their last piece of bread. They may have been few in number, but they offer sufficient proof that everything can be taken from a man but one thing: the last of the human freedoms—to choose one's attitude in any given set of circumstances, to choose one's own way."[7]

Two men looked out from
Prison bars.
One saw mud,
One saw stars.

What are you seeing at the moment?

For Reflection and Discussion

1. What, in your life right now, is that "bur" in your sock? Why is it so difficult to *choose* a good attitude when negative emotions swirl? What works best for you at those times?

2. Do you agree that "the way you think about a situation *before* you enter it will greatly affect its outcome"? If so, what are some practical applications of this truth?

3. What encouragement do you draw from the story of Paul and Silas in prison?

4. Which of the "sanctifiers" is most needed in you or your ministry team these days? Why?

5. Jot the names of three people who need a little encouragement this week. Write them notes and provide some hope to their day!

Endnotes

1. Charles R. Swindoll, *Strengthening Your Grip*, audiocassette.

2. Swindoll, *Strengthening Your Grip* audiocassette, citing Douglas Colligan, "That Helpless Feeling: The Dangers of Stress," New York magazine (July 14, 1975), 28.

3. The information offered here about Albert Ellis and his REBT theory was gleaned from the Albert Ellis Institute homepage on the Internet, at www.rebt.org/index.html, accessed September 3, 2001. Please note: REBT is not hereby endorsed—but "choosing one's attitude" is a biblical principle and fully recommended!

4. Blaine Allen, *Before You Quit: When Ministry Is Not What You Thought* (Grand Rapids, MI: Kregel Publications, 2001), 57.

5. John Maxwell, *Four Skills Seminary Never Taught Me*, audiocassette, tape 1.

6. Victor Frankl, *Man's Search for Meaning*, (New York: Pocket Books, 1984), 33-34.

7. Frankl, *Man's Search for Meaning*, 86-87.

SIX

→What's Really Inside?

They walked into my office, yelling at the top of their lungs—not at me, at each other.

And they weren't my kids either. They were two grown women who had recently started serving in a program we'd just started at our church.

I took another nervous sip from the glass of Pepsi on my desk, not knowing exactly how to handle this situation. It was my second year serving in ministry, and I hadn't taken the "One Leader Is Yelling at Another Leader—and How to Stop It" class in college. When we all calmed down a bit, I went for the obvious approach and asked this question: "Ladies, if we bumped this glass, what would come out?"

"Well, obviously, Pepsi would come out."

"That's true; if you bump a glass of Pepsi, Pepsi will flow out. So the next question is, What happens when *we* get 'bumped'? What happens when we get skipped over for the promotion? What happens when someone cuts in front of us on the freeway? What happens when our ministry plans are interrupted by someone else's agenda?"

The three of us talked about that for several minutes until we all held hands and sang a chorus of Kumbayah. (Well, at least it resolved the conflict.) But here is the question: What attitude spills out when *you* get bumped?

What Am I Spreading?

Yes, it helps to remember what flows out when we get bumped. According to the Bible, "out of the overflow of the heart the mouth speaks" (Matthew 12:34b). So what are we putting into our minds and our hearts that later surfaces in our attitudes? It's an important question, because whatever is inside of us is going to spill out and spread onto others every time we're just a little bit jostled.

> Whatever is inside of us is going to spill out and spread onto others every time we're just a little bit jostled.

And the spillage can spread quickly. I can remember a time my wife, Mary, and I were on the freeway, and all of a sudden, at a time traffic shouldn't be stopping, we stopped.

Dead stop—no movement except for people getting out of their cars. Now, I don't mind if I'm driving in circles, not going anywhere, as long as I'm moving. But to sit there is just painful for me. So we sat there for almost two hours, my attitude sinking from bad to worse.

I'm talking and I'm upset; Mary keeps trying to bring me back with, "Maybe someone's hurt." I'm just thinking of myself, and everything's directed inward. I'm getting mad.

About two hours later, we finally moved past the scene where an accident had been cleared from the road.

I said, "That's it, we're late, and we're going back home."

We turned around, and after two hours Mary began to develop a bad attitude. She started shooting back, and we had a little "disagreement" in the car.

That surprised me.

But why should it? I have said in the previous chapter that attitudes are our choice. And this is true. However, I need to also let you know that *attitudes are transferable.* The reason? Pure erosion. The Bible reminds us: "Whoever walks with wise people will be wise, but whoever associates with fools will suffer" (Proverbs 13:20, GWT). My wife's attitude began to slip a bit because she was sitting next to an idiot for almost two hours. Bad company corrupts good character, as I Corinthians 15:33, reminds us.

Look at it like this: My wife is an avid gardener and has every gardening tool under the sun. If I had my way, I would just cement over everything. I just like washing down cement; it seems easier. Because we've gone with her approach, our landscaping is beautiful. She uses many different tools to plant, cultivate, and prune. So here's how I view it from the perspective of my wife's gardening tools: *Am I going to be a cultivator or a hoe in my life today?*

A cultivator has three prongs on it and has been designed to break up the soil around a plant to make more oxygen available, as well as to blend in fertilizer and to keep the ground loose so that water can get to the roots. Cultivation stirs up the ground and makes it ready for seed, ready for growth.

But a hoe scrapes the dirt and pushes obstacles aside. It cuts and uproots in one pull. Both tools were created with a specific purpose; both are useful instruments. One cultivates, the other scrapes. So it is with our attitude. We make a choice to

(attitude)

> We can end up scraping away the person-hood—the individual needs, the concerns, and all the little bothersome hurts—to "get things done."

either plow up the soil with the kids in our classrooms (and the leaders who minister to them), or we can scrape away the seeds that have been planted and uproot previous growth with one swift move of our attitude. We can end up scraping away the person-hood—the individual needs, the concerns, and all the little bothersome hurts—to "get things done."

Who will come in contact with me today, and how will I affect them? Will they be *nurtured* or *leveled* by my attitudes?

What does this say to you about the importance of your own attitude in your children's ministry, no matter how or where you serve?

The Bible can help you become a cultivator. Here's a good "top three" list to get you started. Notice that all of these verses are "others directed," and many deal with our nonverbal attitudes:

An anxious heart weighs a man down, but a kind word cheers him up. —Proverbs 12:25

All the days of the oppressed are wretched, but the cheerful heart has a continual feast. —Proverbs 15:15

A cheerful look brings joy to the heart, and good news gives health to the bones. —Proverbs 15:30

The bottom line on attitude and how it affects our ministry is summed up in this statement that I consistently recall to my staff: *Every staff member, leader, and volunteer in our ministry is the church in the mind of a non-Christian.* Our attitude, for the most part, gives this impression to the visitor.

Let's make sure our hearts are filled with the right things, because out of the heart that's bumped, flows whatever is inside. How will we know whether we are contagious with good and helpful attitudes? Perhaps we will never know, but one way we recognize who has influenced us for the good over the years is to hold people in our minds for a moment and notice what feelings well up inside us. Why not try that right now? Think back to some of the people you've known and worked with over the years. What impressions do you have? What feelings bubble up?

Remember: Attitudes are contagious. You are "infecting" people daily—for better or worse!

What Am I Reflecting?

I'd like to change the analogy a bit here in the middle of this chapter. You see, just as attitude is contagious—it can spill out on others like Pepsi from a glass; it can spew out from our bodies like germs from a bad cold—there is another kind of "influencing effect" that comes packaged with our attitude. It reflects, or projects, onto others just as a light we might shine on someone by tilting a mirror to the sun.

Consider Webster's definition of a mirror: any smooth or polished object whose surface reflects light and images; a true portrayal or representation.

> The mirror doesn't lie, but you can change the way you look—from the inside out.

We are mirrors. We reflect. And most of us would benefit by changing at least some aspect of the way we reflect our attitude, day by day. The mirror doesn't lie, but you can change the way you look—from the inside out.

Consider this verse:

The Lord said to Samuel, "Don't look at how handsome Eliab is or how tall he is, because I have not chosen him. God does not see the same way people see. People look at the outside of a person, but the LORD looks at the heart." —I Samuel 16:7, NCV

"How can I change my reflection?" you ask. Take one or more of these three actions—having to do with angle, lighting, and makeup—and you'll see it happen!

→Change Your Angle

The Son reflects the glory of God and shows exactly what God is like. —Hebrews 1:3a, NCV

Notice there are two types of reflection: (1) You reflect yourself by looking directly into the mirror. This shows you the exact representation of who you are. (2) You reflect yourself to others. They see your reflection, but you do not see yourself. For example, when you drive your car, you don't see yourself but you are reflecting yourself to others. Next time you pull up to a light in the middle of an intersection, look in the other driver's rearview mirror. The person in the car ahead of you is reflecting his or her eyes back at you. And if we come to the point of no longer liking what we've been reflecting, we can reach out and change the angle of our mirrors. That is, we can adjust our lifestyle, our way of talking to others, or our basic orientation to daily living.

So, what are we reflecting to parents? to the kids in our ministry? to our co-leaders in ministry? I've found there are at least five "angles of life" that we can reflect to others, attitudes that pull us down and pull others with us. So ask yourself the five questions below when you're considering what kinds of reflections emanate from your own attitude mirror.

I. Am I hassling others with my hurried life? Here's the problem of "just gotta get it done—no matter what, or who, is in the way." I can't describe the problem much better than Robert Kriegel and Louis Patler did, in their book for business managers titled *If It Ain't Broke...Break It!*

You've got the gotta's if…

You are working harder but wondering if you are accomplishing that much more.

(attitude)

You always feel behind...running a little late.

You are more irritable, critical, or short-tempered with the people around you.

You see less and less of your friends and family.

You get more headaches, backaches, stomachaches.

You have a tough time relaxing.

You feel guilty if you aren't working.

It's all work and no play.

You tire easily and feel fatigued.

You sometimes feel depressed or sad without any apparent cause.

You need to be continually busy.[1]

A Promise for the Hurried Life

Let go [of your concerns]! Then you will know that I am God. I rule the nations. I rule the earth.
—Psalm 46:10, GWT

Not surprisingly, research has found that the Type A lifestyle is incredibly stressful. You are much more inflexible, impatient, irritable, and anxious when you're in a hurry. Have you noticed that? As a Type A personality myself, I have. In fact, the hurried lifestyle can literally kill you. The phenomenon has become such a concern in Japan that they actually have a word for it: *karoshi*. It means "death from overwork."

2. Have I reflected defeat with a hopeless life?

A Promise for the Hopeless Life

I know the plans that I have for you, declares the Lord. They are plans for peace and not disaster, plans to give you a future filled with hope.
—Jeremiah 29:11, GWT

Here is someone who's searching but finding no meaning or purpose in life. This can happen even when we're serving in ministry. We come to the place of feeling, deep inside, "What's the point?"

When we deliberately live each day in the recognition of God's presence, drawing from him the hope and meaning we need, we can hardly reflect defeat. No matter the circumstances, our hope remains solid, based solely on his promises.

3. Have I added to the work with a heavy life?

Do you feel as if you're always shouldering a great, heavy burden? You may indeed have a lot of responsibility. So a sense of heaviness can overwhelm you in children's ministry.

In contrast to the hopeless person, who is overwhelmed with the seeming meaninglessness of the work, this person is overwhelmed with the sheer *amount* of the work.

A few weekends ago, a group of children started crying in our toddler room. Can you imagine seven or eight little kids hollering their lungs out, all at the same time? Life can get a little heavy in the toddler room. But when I poked my head in, the men and women working there had huge smiles on their faces. *What a contrast,* I thought.

Yet I know those smiles where being imprinted on the souls of each of the children, week by week, even when the kids took a little time out to cry.

Yes, we all get tired. But the Lord of the universe dwells in us! Let's draw from his strength. I'm quite certain this is the only strength that kept someone like John Wesley, the founder of the Methodist Church, going strong, even as he approached ninety years old. During his lifetime of almost ninety years, spanning from 1703 to 1791, Wesley

→traveled some 4,500 miles each year (on horseback) and preached an average of twice daily (often outdoors) in fifty years of ministry;

→wrote on theology, medicine, and other topics—now collected in more than thirty-two volumes;

→wrote letters and journals that fill nine volumes, with the letters alone numbering around 2,600![2]

Talk about the strength of the Lord. Listen to what Wesley said when he entered his fifties: "The more I use my strength, the more I have. I am often much tired the first time I preach in a day; a little the second time; but after the third or fourth, I rarely feel either weakness or weariness."[3]

Wesley surely relied upon God for his strength. That means something special to each individual believer. For each of us, it means not being driven by our own needs but being calmly, peacefully open to taking each step as God opens the way before us. The primary way to confront the heavy life, then, is to stay in a state of awareness of God's presence.

4. Do I spark overreactions with my own overheated life?

This is the "I am ready to snap" life. Some of us reflect it every day. Little things are really *big* things to us.

In February 1990, the Los Angeles Bomb Squad received a call about a suspicious pickup truck parked downtown. They checked it out and found four hundred pounds of explosives packed into several fifty-five-gallon drums. Had the bomb been detonated, it would have blown a crater seventy feet wide and twenty feet deep.[4]

A man was arrested for the attempted bombing. Why was this man on such a horrible incendiary mission? Well, the bombs were all in or near the IRS building. It turns out that the man believed the IRS owed him money, and he wasn't going to leave them alone until he got the money.

The amount he believed they owed him? Fourteen dollars. A heated life sometimes shows itself through overreaction. No, you're not ready to bomb anything, but are you occasionally lobbing a few verbal grenades here and there? What about the napalm-blaster looks you give your family members when they won't let you concentrate on lesson preparation late on a Saturday night? And how about your "subtle" guerrilla tactics when it comes to making sure that church politics, if there were such a thing, go your way?

5. Am I draining others' energies because of my hollow life?

We're running on empty. The car is out of gas. But it's hard to steer a parked car. Suffering a severe lack of energy, enthusiasm, and passion for the ministry, we walk around as hollow shells, making sure no one can tell we've lost our first love.

But people *can* tell. Maybe not consciously; nevertheless, your hollowness will reflect and influence every person around you. The solution? Apply for vacation time. Go on retreat, or go with your family. But go.

Renew. Refresh.

Open yourself to God's strength once again.

In contrast to these unhealthy and destructive reflections, we want to reflect a *healthy* life. How do we do it? Reflect the things of God, not the circumstances around you. Change your angle and reflect the Son!

And we pray this in order that you may live a life worthy of the Lord and may please him in every way: bearing fruit in every good work, growing in the knowledge of God. —Colossians 1:10

→Change Your Lighting

As water shows you your face, so your mind shows you what kind of person you are. —Proverbs 27:19, ICB

The second way to change your reflection is to adjust the lighting. What are some things that dim our light as we serve in children's ministry? things that may cast a shadow? Consider:

→Crying children

→Children who won't listen

→Children who won't follow directions

→Too many children and not enough leaders

→Constantly changing programs and curriculum

→Realizing that your joy has left you

→No focus, no mission, and no purpose

→Lack of values to guide your ministry

I have to be honest and say that sometimes these things really bum me out. When these kinds of things get to me, I am reminded that it's time to change my lighting. I am not in the light but in the shadows. Meditate on this verse for a moment:

> **Here is the message we have heard from God and now tell to you: God is light, and in him there is no darkness at all. So if we say that we have fellowship with God, but we continue living in darkness, then we are liars. We do not follow the truth. God is in the light. We should live in the light, too. If we live in the light, we share fellowship with each other. And when we live in the light, the blood of the death of Jesus, God's Son, is making us clean from every sin.** —I John 1:5-7, ICB

Sometimes we walk in our own light:

> **But instead, some of you want to light your own fires and make your own light. So, go, walk in the light of your fires, and trust your own light to guide you. But this is what you will receive from me: You will lie down in a place of pain.** —Isaiah 50:11, NCV

How can we walk in God's light instead of the light of our own fires? Among other things we can do, perhaps the most effective is to stay immersed in the Word of God. Most often, when we find we are walking in shadows and our reflection is dimmed, we've lost our contact with the source of the light. In this regard, think about the top five signs that you're not reading your Bible enough:

1. You think Abraham, Isaac, and Jacob may have had a few hits in the seventies.

2. You think "hallucinations" is a book of the Bible.

3. You are frustrated because Charlton Heston is not listed in the table of contents under "Moses."

4. When someone says, "Turn to Mark,"—you ask the guy next to you his name.

5. Your favorite Old Testament character is Bob the tomato.

Seriously, are you staying in the Word these days? If not, you are wandering in the shadows.

→Change Your Makeup

> **For if you just listen and don't obey, it is like looking at your face in a mirror but doing nothing to improve your appearance. You see yourself, walk away, and forget what you look like. But if you keep looking steadily into God's perfect law—the law that sets you free—and if you do what it says and don't forget what you heard, then God will bless you for doing it.** —James 1:23-25, NLT

(attitude)

My wife tells me that women typically use makeup in one of two ways: (1) to cover up blemishes, and (2) to enhance facial features. So ask yourself:

→ Have I been using excuses to cover up blemishes in my life?

→ Have I been enhancing my life and look with God's Word?

→ What do I need to enhance in my life this week to better reflect God to others?

You may be thinking at this point, *Craig, it's helpful to know how to keep my own attitude right, but my problem these days is that I'm trying to get others to change. How can I do that, when they seem so opposed to budging the least bit?*

I agree that so much of ministry is trying to *persuade* others. Our attitude and approach are critical in this, determining what we are going to draw out of people. Therefore, I'd like to tell you about something that can work to help bring a change to your own attitude and that of others. It works both ways. Emory Griffin, a psychology professor at Wheaton College, has called it the "Foot-in-the-Door" approach.

He basically says that sometimes when we're asking ourselves or others to change radically, it's too much to expect a complete turnaround all at once. Therefore, we use an incremental approach, step by small step (a journey of a thousand miles begins with one small step). To test the effectiveness of such an approach, some social researchers did a study.

The researchers selected a number of homes at random and made personal visits to the residents. They claimed to represent an environmental group that was erecting billboards that said, "KEEP CALIFORNIA BEAUTIFUL." They asked whether the homeowners would be willing to display this sign on their front lawns. To ensure residents fully understood the request, they showed them a picture of a similar house with the sign in front.

It was really quite funny. Here's an ugly 6x10-foot billboard defacing the property while urging others to beautify the state. The idea that anybody would actually choose to put up such a monstrosity seemed patently ridiculous. And it was—no one accepted the offer.

The researchers used a two-step procedure with another group of homeowners to test the Foot-in-the-Door technique. They first went to the residents with small 3x5-inch cards and asked people to stick the cards in their windows. The cards contained the same appeal for state beautification. Because the behavioral cost of displaying the modest sign was low, many people did it. This left the door open to a much larger request later on. A few weeks later, the callers came back to the folks who had accepted the small signs. They presented their request for permission to put up the huge billboard. Although the majority of the people refused, quite a few agreed to take the large signs.[5]

How can we explain this difference? Griffin says the simplest answer is that the folks who installed the first message *began to view themselves differently*. In other words, they became observers of their own behavior, just as others would observe it. Looking at themselves, they saw people concerned about the environment, who had already let their neighbors know—with the little signs—that they thought it important to keep the state beautiful. In effect, they were reminded of their commitment by taking that first small step. Every time they looked at the little signs in their windows, they were reminded of *who they are*.

Evaluating Your Attitude-Contagion Level

As you know, attitudes are contagious. But what are people catching from you? To find out, try this: Take a survey of people who know you or work with you (or live in your household!). Ask them to write the top ten positive attitudes people tend to catch from you and the top ten negative attitudes people tend to catch from you.

Feel free to make your own entries, too, if you know about some of the things you're "spreading." (Yes, it will be difficult for people to jot things in the negative column. But encourage them to do so while you turn your attention elsewhere. Tell folks that this is an exercise in self-improvement—motivated by the Holy Spirit.)

When you've completed your list, offer thanks to God for the positive influence you have! Then think about how you might remedy the negative attitudes so that you become more of a cultivator than a hoe.

NEGATIVE ATTITUDES

_____

_____

_____

_____

_____

_____

_____

_____

_____

_____

_____

_____

_____

_____

_____

So, if they were already so committed, it would be easier for them to accept a larger role, a bigger act of commitment in erecting the larger sign. "What we have here would be called persuasion through self-perception," says Griffin. "A person becomes convinced by watching his own action."[6]

Your own actions "reflect" back to yourself! Your attitudes (and those of others) can be more easily changed with constant, incremental feedback as positive steps are taken. The secret lies in not expecting too much at the beginning. If you're dissatisfied with your attitude and you know you need to change, just make a start, a small commitment, a first step. Bring another along with you. Begin. You will create the impetus to take the next step, and the next, and the next...

What Will I Do Now?

When we spread attitude, when we reflect attitude, our attempts to do it right will be severely tested. How will we respond?

I think of an event that took place on a cold, icy December night way back in 1914. It occurred in the life of Thomas Edison, the famous inventor of yesteryear, and is adapted here from Selfhelp Magazine online.[7] We have him to thank, by the way, for the phonograph and for talking movies, for the microphone, and the incandescent light. In fact, Edison left us myriad inventions before he died.

But that night was a tragic one, during a period in which Edison was balancing himself on a financial tightrope. Suddenly, the word "Fire!" echoed throughout the plant where he'd been working.

His daughter ran up to Edison as he was watching the blaze—which apparently was beyond control. Instead of showing panic or despair, he calmly directed his daughter to get her mother and their friends. He wasn't looking for sympathy or volunteers to fight the fire. Rather, he wanted to make sure that they saw the spectacle. "They'll never see another fire like this as long as they live," he remarked.

The next day, when the fire was finally subdued, he told his employees, "We're rebuilding." He directed them to get the equipment to tear down the old building and begin again. Near the end of his instruction, Edison nonchalantly remarked, "Oh, by the way. Anybody know where we can get some money?"

Can you give your worries and cares to the Lord right now? If you do, you'll open your heart to a peace that passes all understanding. It will fill you up, more and more. And when you get bumped, guess what will spill out all over the fortunate soul who jostled you?

For Reflection and Discussion

1. Have you been bumped lately? What came out? Do you need to ask someone for forgiveness?

2. As you've worked in the garden of your ministry during the past few weeks, have you been mostly cultivating or hoeing?

3. In your group, talk about this concept: "Attitudes are transferable." What positive and negative transfers have been occurring among you during the past year?

4. As honestly as you can, answer the key question in this chapter: *What am I reflecting?* If your group feels ready and comfortable doing so, spend time giving one another some feedback about this.

5. Which is most needed in your ministry team at present: a change of angle, a change of lighting, or a change of makeup? Talk about the problems, and brainstorm for some practical solutions.

Endnotes

1. Robert Kriegel and Louis Patler, *If It Ain't Broke...Break It!* (New York: Warner Books, 1991), 54.

2. Erwin Paul Rudolph, ed., *The John Wesley Treasury* (Wheaton, IL: Victor Books, 1979), 10-11.

3. Rudolph, *The John Wesley Treasury*, 75-76.

4. Kendall, John, et al., "Bomb-Laden Truck Defused on Westside," The Los Angeles Times (Feb. 23, 1990).

5. Emory A. Griffin, *The Mind Changers: The Art of Christian Persuasion* (Wheaton, IL: Tyndale House Publishers, 1980), 189-190.

6. Griffin, *The Mind Changers: The Art of Christian Persuasion*, 190.

7. "Meditative Thoughts: Determination," in Selfhelp Magazine, an online publication, found at www.shpm.com/articles/stress/meditate/determ5.html, accessed September 3, 2001.

TEAMWORK

"*two are better than one, because they have a good return for their work: If one falls down, his friend can help him up. But pity the man who falls and has no one to help him up!*"

—Ecclesiastes 4:9-10

SEVEN

→Three Are Better Than Two

What a marvel San Francisco's Golden Gate Bridge is! Just consider one aspect of this engineering marvel: the cables. At the south end of the bridge, a cross-section of one of the two main cables is open to public view. When you look at it, you think, "Wow, that's one honkin' cable!"

The diameter is slightly more than thirty-six inches. The length is 7,650 feet. But it gets even more interesting. There are 27,572 wires in each of those cables, with a total length that could stretch for 80,000 miles (more than three trips around the earth).

I like to think of a cable like that as a perfect illustration of teamwork. If we gather small groups or large groups of people, let them wrap together and form a bond in the unity of the Spirit, they become like the individual wires that make up the strands that make up a large cable. They move as one; they have the strength of many.

The weight of the main cables in the Golden Gate Bridge totals 24,500 tons, which means the bridge carries the suspension weight of 49 million pounds—all hanging by two megacables. The reason the bridge can stand, and can carry the weight of multitudes of vehicles, is because of a biblical principle uttered centuries ago:

> **Two are better than one, because they have a good return for their work: If one falls down, his friend can help him up. But pity the man who falls and has no one to help him up! Also, if two lie down together, they will keep warm. But how can one keep warm alone? Though one may be overpowered, two can defend themselves. A cord of three strands is not quickly broken.**
> —Ecclesiastes 4:9-12

I've seen videos of earthquakes trying to bring down the Golden Gate Bridge. I've seen that bridge swinging and twisting and warping. But it doesn't break, it doesn't bend, and it doesn't fall because 27,572 strands hang tough—together.

So, how many "strands" are in your ministry team? Are you hanging together? And are you supporting the weight equally so that one person isn't bearing the entire load?

Take a Cue From the Master

I'd like to make some observations about teamwork before we jump into analyzing the characteristics of a dynamic team. So think with me for a moment: *What was Jesus' attitude toward working in teamwork with others?*

Luke 9 records one of Jesus' mind-blowing miracles: "Late in the afternoon the Twelve came to him and said, 'Send the crowd away so they can go to the surrounding villages and countryside and find food and lodging, because we are in a remote place here.' He replied, 'You give them something to eat.' They answered, 'We have only five loaves of bread and two fish—unless we go and buy food for all this crowd.' (About five thousand men were there.) But he said to his disciples, 'Have them sit down in groups of about fifty each'" (Luke 9:12-14).

> Even Jesus modeled teamwork with his disciples. It wasn't as though he couldn't have done it all by himself!

Now we know that Jesus took the five loaves and two fish, looked up to heaven, and blessed the food. He broke the loaves apart and gave the disciples portions with which to feed the crowd. He kept giving and giving and giving, until the people had eaten as much as they wanted. Then when they picked up all the leftovers, there were twelve baskets full—more food than they originally brought to the picnic.

If you read through the New Testament, you'll find that many of Jesus' miracles were performed with others playing "supporting roles" or contributing to the event in some way. In fact, Jesus involved people in almost every miracle. In faith, the people called out to Jesus, or were brought to him. At the very least, he encouraged them to have more faith or asked them what they wanted.

In this instance in Luke 9, too, the disciples were involved in the process. They came to Jesus with the request, and then he sent them into the crowd to get it done. Even Jesus modeled teamwork with his disciples. It wasn't as though he couldn't have done it all by himself!

Teams have more creative potential than individuals. Pooling all resources to complete a task usually means the task gets done more efficiently and more effectively. One of my colleagues on a former church staff used to say, "All of us are smarter than one of us." Inventor Henry Ford said it like this: "Coming together is a beginning; keeping together is progress; working together is a success."[1]

Go Ahead, Be Dynamic!

Come with me back to the desert of the ancient Middle East. When the Hebrews loaded up the family trucksters and headed onto the interstate pursued by Egyptian chariots, they ended up in the desert with Moses leading the entire caravan. After

(teamwork)

forty years of "applied map reading," they were no closer to finding the "Exit" sign that they were looking for (something like, "Promised Land Ahead—Food, Lodging").

When Moses passed on, he gave the reigns of leadership to a man named Joshua. Finally, the hundreds of thousands of Hebrews were getting ready to take the Promised Land exit, but under new leadership. The new leader was giving new kinds of orders—to bring them all together and get them all on the same page:

> **So Joshua ordered the officers of the people: "Go through the camp and tell the people, 'Get your supplies ready. Three days from now you will cross the Jordan here to go in and take possession of the land the Lord your God is giving you for your own.'"** —Joshua 1:10-11

How did the people take to Joshua's team-building efforts?

> **Then they answered Joshua, "Whatever you have commanded us we will do, and wherever you send us we will go. Just as we fully obeyed Moses, so we will obey you. Only may the Lord your God be with you as he was with Moses. Whoever rebels against your word and does not obey your words, whatever you may command them, will be put to death. Only be strong and courageous!"** —Joshua 1:16-18

I'd like to suggest that in this brief passage, we have the building blocks for creating a dynamic team. Think about it:

→ "Whatever you have commanded us we will do."
That's *cooperation.*

→ "Wherever you send us we will go."
That's *flexibility.*

→ "Just as we fully obeyed Moses, so we will obey you."
That's *commitment.*

→ "Whoever rebels against your word and does not obey your words, whatever you may command them, will be put to death."
That's *loyalty.*

→ "Only be strong and courageous!"
That's *encouragement.*

So in Joshua 1:16-18, we find these five characteristics of a dynamic team. Through exercising these qualities, the Israelites successfully gained entrance to the Promised Land. Let's learn from them about what makes a dynamic team in our ministries today.

I. Dynamic Teams Advance Unity.

Jesus prayed in John 17:21, "that all of them may be one, Father, just as you are in me and I am in you."

I don't know whether you've ever tuned a piano, but if you have three pianos sounding discordant, a professional will use a tuning fork to set the tension of the first string on one of the pianos. Then when he's through tuning all the strings on that piano, he'll strike the tuning fork again to begin work on the second piano. Similarly, he'll use the fork once again as he begins tuning the third piano.

The point is, he won't tune one piano and then tune the subsequent ones in relation to the first. No, he'll start each one with the perfect pitch of the tuning fork, because of this mathematical axiom: *things equal to the same thing are equal to one another.* That's the way we are as team members. Jesus Christ dwells in each of us. God's Spirit unifies us and gives us the spiritual "harmony" we need. We may be from different cultures, have different likes and dislikes, live by different internal rules, and express vastly differing personalities, but because we are all "struck to the same pitch"—the Spirit of Christ within us—we have unity in him. Our job then is to cooperate on the practical level, in the daily matters of carrying out our ministry together. We advance the unity by advancing the kingdom, hand in hand, contributing our unique gifts as needed, and encouraging and supporting one another all along the way.

> God's Spirit unifies us and gives us the spiritual "harmony" we need.

I once read about some college students who had a final exam looming on a Monday morning. They decided to get away and study together in the mountains during the weekend. They took their books and notes and charts and time lines—and blew off the final. They decided to hike and ski instead.

They came back down from the hills on Wednesday—two days too late—and told the professor a little story they'd invented, which went something like this: "You see, we were up in the mountains on our way back, blew a tire, stopped and fixed it, and things just went from bad to worse." There was also something about a blizzard and the lack of a spare and emergency lodging in a farmhouse. It was really tough.

The professor said there was no problem and that he'd love to give them the exam anyway. So he put the students in separate rooms and handed out the test. The first question was easy, for ten points: "What is your name?"

They turned the page and scanned the second question, which was also short and sweet, but for ninety points: "Which tire?"

When we're on a dynamic team, we constantly seek to cooperate. It demands knowing and appreciating one another's stories. It means staying in close contact, with lots of give-and-take, so that the awesome reality of our spiritual unity becomes the powerful reality of our practical working relationships.

2. Dynamic Teams "Flex" to Meet Changing Needs.

If you fish, you know that you occasionally hook a heavy, wiggling catch at the end of the line. Even if you don't fish, you've no doubt observed how a fishing rod bends without breaking. Similarly, dynamic teams have to change to meet needs, to bend without breaking.

Why is this true? Because all teams, at some point, face adversity. And the key to dealing with it effectively is *flexibility*. A team member may leave. Or a team member may choose not to remain loyal to the mission any longer. But in each case, good teams will stretch through the hard times.

I opened this chapter talking about an awesome bridge and its teamwork-demonstrating cables. Another great bridge can supply us with a good demonstration of flexibility: Japan's Akashi Kaikyo Bridge. It's the longest suspension bridge in the world today. In fact, the cable approaches three miles long (12,828 feet), and a cross-section has 290 minicable strands, each strand with 127 wires making up each main cable. The bridge spans the water over one of the most earthquake-prone areas of the world.

A few years ago, in 1995, there was a 7.2-level earthquake—the Kobe earthquake—near the bridge. Although the bridge wasn't damaged, some interesting things happened to it, the most surprising being that *the main span is now almost four feet longer than it was before!*

That's right, as a result of the earth parting beneath the span, one of the tower trestles came several inches off axis, while the other moved several inches off axis in the opposite direction. The result, in round figures, a bridge that had been about 12,828 feet in length became a bridge now almost 12,832 feet in length. Four feet longer than before. Why? When it was hit with adversity, it stretched to meet the demand placed on it.

When hit with adversity, does your ministry team stretch to meet the demand placed on it? When you're working together with your peers in ministry, no matter what you're doing, when adversity comes, are you stretching to meet the demands placed on the team? You may ask, "Why hang a bridge? Why make a bridge flexible?" The obvious reason is that when a cement bridge is hit with adversity, it will crash. That's why cables are used instead of cement. If this bridge had been built with just straight cement, with no flexibility, it would have come tumbling down. But when the opportunity and the adversity came, the bridge still functioned very well. It's just four feet longer.

3. Dynamic Teams Stay Focused.

They say that if you try to chase two rabbits, both will escape. We need to be focused on what we're doing, chasing just one rabbit at a time. In 1998, we launched our mission statement for our children's ministry here at Saddleback. We put All STARS in motion: sharing, teaming, advancing, recognizing, surrendering. We're committed to these five things—the purposes of evangelism, fellowship, discipleship, service, and worship. We're getting the word out that these things are essential to what our children's ministry is. Now we're designing our process for maturing in the faith—programs that will help children grow deeper in the spiritual walk. How can we accomplish that? Only through the ability of all our team members and volunteer leaders staying focused on the same thing.

World-renowned business writer Peter F. Drucker, a leading expert on organization and management principles, says that when you find your vision becoming unfocused, you should ask yourself a number of diagnostic questions:

➔ "What would happen if this were *not* done at all?" (If the answer is "Nothing," then stop doing it!)

→ "Which of the activities in my [calendar] could be done by somebody else just as well, if not better?" (Delegate it!)

→ "Am I wasting the time of my staff [or team] members?" (Go ahead—just ask them!)

→ "What time-wasters flow from a lack of a system or lack of foresight?" (Look for the recurring crisis!)

→ "Am I attending [too many] meetings?" (Remember: You can't meet and work at the same time!)[2]

As you answer these questions for yourself, and as a ministry team, you'll begin focusing on your focus. Don't let any rabbits escape!

4. In Dynamic Teams, the Members Value One Another.

We'll talk about this in depth in Chapter II, but for now let me say that it's really all about loyalty.

There is, in this life, probably no more admirable quality of team or friendship than personal loyalty. It displays how much we value one another.

Are you loyal to every team member and the vision you've committed to? It's a staying force. Occasionally a team will break down because something discussed within the group leaks out to other seemingly interested parties; we call this gossip. Things may be said that encourage disunity among team members. The traditional topic of these types of discussions is *you*, the leader.

And this is unacceptable. It devalues the other members.

> A breach of trust is so difficult to overcome among team members.

One of our *guiding principles* here in our children's ministry at Saddleback is affirming, honoring, and valuing others through authentic leadership. We go directly to one another if we have something to discuss. If a team member cannot practice this type of behavior, he or she is encouraged to seek another ministry opportunity. Why? Because a breach of trust is so difficult to overcome among team members. I didn't say impossible, but very difficult.

5. Dynamic Teams Play Together.

This is my favorite, because it's a fantastic way of generating a spirit of encouragement within a group. Remember the "Out of the Box" activities I mentioned previously? The reason we do these activities is to just get out of our rut. Playing together is a positive experience that ought to stretch the boundaries of creativity. But to play together and encourage one another, we may have to make a dent in our tightly crafted work schedules. Are you willing to make those tough choices for the sake of team health?

Along with the OOTBs, another thing we do on our team is hand out a teamwork jersey to one of the members every two weeks. It's a baseball jersey that says "TEAMWORK" across the front and "CHILDREN'S MINISTRY" with the number "I" on the back. The person who receives it is the one who has best exemplified teamwork to unify the team. The person who had the jersey previously signs it and gives it to the new owner, explaining why he or she was chosen. This is just one ritual we do to invite a culture that values team.

Take Time to Offer Encouragement

Opportunities abound for lending encouragement wherever we are. Every day, in all our interactions, either in the family, at work, or at church, we face the choice of building up or tearing down. In fact, our attitude toward others *actually shapes what they become.* Have you ever thought of it this way?

The Bible tells us to "encourage one another and build each other up" (I Thessalonians 5:11a). The Bible says that a kind word brings joy to the heart, and that we are to speak only "what is helpful for building others up according to their needs, that it may benefit those who listen" (Ephesians 4:29b). Can you see why encouragement is so important? It's what we need if we're going to have dynamic teamwork.

So, where are you now with *your* team? When you send out a memo asking for more work, do you include a word of affirmation about another job already well done? When you must offer critique, can you also offer a word of thanks?

Not too long ago, two men were taking a coffee break at work. One guy always complained about how much money it took to raise his son—the cost of clothes, insurance, braces, gifts, $20 here, $20 there, the whole thing. Finally, after several months, the other man said, "You know, my wife and I haven't spent a dime on our son since he was killed in a car wreck four years ago."

In light of all your blessings, what do you need to say thank you for? Who do you need to say thank you to? People blossom under affirmation, and they wilt under criticism. Every time you appreciate the people around you, you raise their value, you honor them, you build the team, and you build the kingdom.

PRACTICAL PATHWAY

Maintaining Team Health

I t's great to be part of a dynamic children's ministry team—or to lead one. But even the best of teams need "maintenance" if they're to retain high levels of influence for the kingdom. Do you know what to do to keep your team at optimum performance levels?

According to Kenneth Blazier and Linda Isham in *The Teaching Church at Work*, "Task-oriented groups tend to neglect group maintenance. The usual tendency is to assume something like this: 'We have a job to do; our time is limited; let's get on with it.'"[3] But we need to pay attention to the *life of the group itself*, not just the job it does. In fact, the health of the group's life is critical to a group's functioning. You can care for your team's maintenance needs in these ways:

Constantly clarify expectations.

Your team needs to feel belonging and ownership. Each member's role is vital. If a person doesn't show up or drops the ball, it affects the whole team and ministry. If team members understand they are essential and know they are accountable to others, apathy won't have room to develop.

Discuss or think over the following questions:

➜What are some of the unclear expectations around here?

➜What are some of the "performance standards" we use to evaluate our work?

➜What first steps can we take to clear up some of the confusion?

Provide information and training in basic group skills.

This includes such things as how to listen, ask questions, summarize, deal with differences of opinion, relieve tension, and resolve conflict.

Discuss or think over the following questions:

➜What forms of training have we enjoyed recently?

➜What do people still want to learn and to practice?

➜What plans can we make for future training modules?

Allow time for personal sharing.

Knowing that others care lightens individual burdens and concerns. The team will have a greater sense of unity when members show they care about one another, not just about the assigned tasks.

Discuss or think over the following questions:

→How much do we know about one another? How can we pray for one another?

→Does our typical meeting format allow for sharing? If not, what would we like to add?

Always affirm God's presence.

Your team probably begins each meeting with prayer. However, the routine of praying before you get started can result in rote recitation rather than meaningful communication with God. Instead of always opening with prayer, you could have team members take turns leading the group in affirming God's presence. Team members could lead the group in a time of guided prayer and reflection, a few songs of worship, or in reading Scriptures of praise and thanks. Starting your meeting with affirming God's presence in a meaningful way will help your team stay focused on our ultimate purpose and goal. (These thoughts on maintaining team health are adapted from Blazier and Isham.)[4]

Discuss or think over the following questions:

→How important is prayer in this group? Why?

→To what extent do we trust in God's power to make this ministry effective? What evidence do we have?

→What can we do in the future to encourage greater awareness of God among us?

Suggestion for Group Application:

Why not set aside an entire afternoon or evening for group maintenance? The discussion questions listed here could take up at least a couple of two-hour sessions—with a snack break in between! Remember to assign someone to jot the major discussion points/issues on chalkboard or newsprint as you go. You'll be able use these notes for your future problem-solving sessions. ■

For Reflection and Discussion

1. If you were to think of your team as a bunch of strands that make up a cable holding up your children's ministry, how many cables would you have as a part of your leadership team? What are their names?

2. Review the five qualities of dynamic teams. Where are your strengths and weaknesses in each of them?

3. How would you evaluate your team unity at present? What still needs to improve in this area?

4. Assess the practical value, to you, of Peter Drucker's diagnostic questions relating to "focus."

5. In your group, brainstorm some ways you could "play" in the future. (First be sure you all agree that this would be valuable!)

Endnotes

1. The Model T Ford Club homepage at http://www.modelt.org/tquotes.html, accessed September 25, 2001.

2. Adapted from Peter F. Drucker, "Time Management," in James D. Berkley, ed., *Leadership Handbooks of Practical Theology, Volume 3: Leadership and Administration* (Grand Rapids, MI: Baker Book House, 1994), 74-75.

3. Kenneth Blazier and Linda Isham, ed., *The Teaching Church at Work* (Valley Forge, PA: Judson Press, 1993), 43.

4. Blazier and Isham, ed., *The Teaching Church at Work*, 43.

EIGHT

→What Are You Saying?

Have you ever been told it would be nice to "deepen the communication levels" in your ministry? Or maybe you were the one making that request. In any event, the statement, which we often hear in one form or another, points out how much we value good communication. Yet so many of us haven't "compared notes" about what good communication actually is. That's why every children's minister and volunteer ought to review the basics.

In the first half of this chapter, I'm going to cover levels of communication, some standard techniques for communicating better, and some ways to increase our ability to directly say what we want. I'll dedicate the rest of the chapter to focus on something extremely important that usually slips by us—the power of our nonverbal signals.

Do You Know the Basics?

One of the reasons we need to hone our communication skills is that, if we don't have good abilities in this area, our interactions with others will likely fall into one of three less-than-optimum frameworks:

1. I win—you lose;

2. I want out, I'll withdraw; or

3. I'll give in to keep things "nice."

We'll deal with the issue of conflict fully in Chapter II, but for now it's enough to realize that the most effective approaches with others have to do with graciously confronting, willingly compromising, and joyfully building consensus. These are the approaches we want as our basic modes of communicating. With that in mind, let's consider the levels we're dealing with when we seek to "deepen" our communication.

Seek the Deep

Most psychologists and other relationship experts will tell you there are at least five levels of verbal interaction. If we were to think in terms of bringing our communication levels to the very "depths" of the ocean (that is, communicating from the depths of our hearts), we could chart things this way:

Level I: Entering the Surf
Content: exchanging routine information
Example: "Pastor, I just finished my remarks about last night's Kid Koncert. It's on your desk."

"Thanks, Bill. I plan to read through it this afternoon."

Level 2: Moving Beyond the Beach
Content: discussing events in others' lives
Example: "Hey, Carlos, did you hear that the Martinez family is vacationing in Switzerland this year?"

"Really? I bet the kids will have a blast!"

Level 3: Diving Under the Waves
Content: offering opinions and ideas
Example: "I think we should have separate rooms for our infants and toddlers. I've seen some of the two-year-olds throwing toys near the cribs, and I don't like that one bit."

"Not a problem, Karissa! Hey, what if we just put a wall in right here? What do you think? Should we raise the issue at the budget meeting?"

(teamwork)

Level 4: Swimming Down to the Depths

Content: sharing feelings and needs

Example: "Sometimes I wish my mom was still around helping me out. I'm really missing her these days, especially when it comes to needing her wisdom about family life."

"Ah! My dad passed away at a young age, too. I'm feeling pretty sad during this holiday season. What was your mom like?"

Level 5: Reaching the Rock-Solid Floor

Content: risking complete transparency

Example: "Hey, Bob, I've got to tell you, even though I'm a church member here, I'm struggling with my marriage these days. It's tearing me up; can you help?"

"Maybe we could form an accountability team—and bring the pastor into it. Anyway…Katie and I have had problems and we worked through it.

Choosing Better Communication

Most of our problems in communicating stem from our reluctance to be direct. After all, this calls for us to bare our souls to some extent, to reveal who we really are. In addition, many of us have been raised to think that being direct is the same as being uncouth or impolite.

Not so. It is always better to state what it is we want, while still remaining gracious and respectful. Then we can listen and reply more effectively. Consider using the following techniques:

→When Confronting, Use "I" Statements.

Clearly, we'll get a much more helpful response by saying, "I'm really feeling hurt by your words" than if we say, "You always attack me with your words!" The first statement is sharing about yourself. (Who can dispute that you're feeling bad?) The second is an attack of the other person's motives. So when you must confront, begin with "I" rather than "You."

→Restate What You Hear, Before You Reply.

When it's important to be clear with one another, try this: Each time the other person makes a point, restate it and ask if you've got it right. Only then will it be best for you to respond. For example, you might say, "I want to be sure I'm hearing you accurately, Calvin. You're saying you feel that I'm ignoring your past accomplishments while piling on the work without enough planning. Is that it?" Now Calvin can say, "No, that's not quite it," and he can state his case more clearly. When you are both sure you're actually hearing each other, the communication keeps going deeper.

> When you are both sure you're actually hearing each other, the communication keeps going deeper.

→Practice Reflecting for Empathy.

Not all communication is of the confrontational variety. Often, in our ministries, we have occasion to hear people's deepest griefs, hurts, and fears. How do we respond?

Many of us react by quickly suggesting a solution or trying to fix the cause of the situation, or simply giving our best advice. Yet when someone is hurting, they usually don't need our advice, at least for now. What they really need is immediate comfort. We can communicate our love and concern nonverbally through touch, eye contact, or offering refreshment. But verbally, it's best to spend the time reflecting their feelings.

What do I mean? It's a technique of hearing the pain and empathizing with it by "saying" that pain (not necessarily their words) back to them. Thus the hurting person can hear it and know you've picked it up in your own heart. For example,

"So you're missing your son who's gone off to college. Is that it?"

"Seems like you're wanting more freedom, huh?"

"You're having some fear about the new job then?"

→Avoid Dirty Fighting Tactics.

Let's face it, there are some ways to "fight fair" and some ways to fight dirty. In any relationship, conflict will surface and we all have our unique responses according to our personalities. Yet we can move through that conflict if we'll avoid a few of the classic, underhanded methods of trying to get the upper hand, such as these:

1. Using gross generalizations. Instead of focusing on the specific problem at hand, you universalize, giving the other person little chance to remedy the situation *as it is.*

   "You're *always* leaving the classrooms in a mess and *never* doing your fair share of cleanup!"

2. Attacking the person instead of the problem. There are solutions to our problems that *do not* involve changing the people in the situation. This is most often the case. Look first to change something in the environment or system to resolve a problem situation. Don't immediately go on the attack, aiming at someone's weaknesses or shortcomings.

   "You know we need to finish up before the bell on Sundays, Jenny. Do you have a problem with telling time or something?"

3. Hauling out all the past grievances. Rather than stick with the problem at hand, you choose to add all the other similar problems that have arisen in the past. This can usually make a pretty big pile! (But it's not going to help solve the problem.)

   "Hey, this isn't the only time! Remember when you...and there was that time...and don't forget when you..."

(teamwork)

4. Making vague accusations. To keep the suspense going—and avoid having to actually reveal your anger—you choose to be the nice guy. You just make some fairly cryptic comments and hope the other person picks up on your grievances.

> "Well, it's probably not that important—about your style of ministry, I mean. Not that you're doing anything particularly wrong, or being incompetent or anything, as far as leading meetings anyway. See you around, man!"

5. Playing one-upmanship. This is the method of taking your hurt, multiplying it by two, and slinging it back at the other person even harder.

> "You think that felt bad? How do you think I felt when you..."

6. Questioning, constantly questioning. This is a way to avoid stating what's really on your mind. You keep the other person guessing about your feelings by shifting the focus back to him or her. However, usually the questions are thinly veiled attacks.

> "Do you really think we have enough staff members for this ministry?"

7. Sinking to sarcasm. This one's not too hard to imagine, because it's often on the tip of our tongues whenever the tensions build. But avoid it like the plague!

> "Yeah, right! You've been just the greatest support to me. I can hardly think of anything you haven't done to help me out with children's church. Please, don't bother doing anything else at all!"

Watch Your Language

Take a minute to think about your team. When you communicate, is someone always trying to "win"? Do you or your teammates take cheap shots that are masked as Christian concern? If so, your team will never reach the rock-solid floor of open and transparent communication. So watch your language. When you build each other up and build trust, your team will be unstoppable in what it can accomplish.

A functioning, trusting, and communicating team will stretch to meet almost any challenge. Your team members will help one another when they fall down, and you'll work *together* to make a difference in the lives of the children you serve. Whatever you do, make sure you and your team keep healthy and building talk going.

What Aren't You Saying?

Maybe you have some room to grow in the area of communication, or maybe your team already communicates better than teenagers in a chat room. Either way, perhaps there is one area you can change to make use of one of the most powerful methods of communication.

We were debriefing an event we'd just held for the kids in our community. It was a huge success, and we were so pleased. We'd jotted a few notes for next year's event and were just about ready to end the meeting. When I asked the team members whether there was anything else that needed to be shared or discussed, one of them said, "Craig, I really appreciated how you just walked around and didn't really get involved with the operational side of things."

I looked around the room to see most, if not all, heads nodding up and down in agreement. Now this was amazing, because my personality typically defaults to "involvement." When I am involved, I have a tendency to get tense or rigid or—controlling. I wasn't involved with their work at this event because *I didn't know what they were doing.* I had other people running the event, and I was outside of the loop.

Being outside the loop allowed for a relaxed, calm, underinvolved feeling. Basically, my whole countenance, body posture, facial muscles, and attitude were pleasant.

> As much as we all know about the importance of good communication, we almost always focus on the speaking part of it.

I walked away from that meeting with one question for myself as it relates to leading a team: *What am I saying when I don't open my mouth?*

Communication is essential to team success, and it involves much more than just words. That's why I've become a student in the college of nonverbal communication. Why? Because as much as we all know about the importance of good communication, we almost always focus on the speaking part of it. Go to any good book on human relations, and you'll find the basics about how to speak and listen effectively. However, as the oddball Kramer said (on the television sitcom *Seinfeld*): "Ninety-four percent of our communication is *nonverbal*, Jerry."

Now not too many of us would consider Kramer an expert on much of anything. But he likely got this one right. And it's a critical recognition for those of us in ministry, because simply *understanding* people is a most basic aspect of *serving* them.

Communicating to one another is the exchange of thoughts or messages by talking, writing, or sending signals. You can hear talking and you can read writing, but can you interpret the signals? Those conscious or inadvertent messages can contribute to making or breaking a ministry team's unity and effectiveness. A shrugged shoulder in response to a question, a crossing of the arms when confronted about a deadline, a curved eyebrow lifted at someone's "brilliant" idea—these actions are communication.

Sending signals and receiving signals—kids are best at it. As adults we typically don't do the "tantrum" dance in the middle of Nordstrom if we can't find our size. We do, however, give off clues that could alert those around us that something's churning inside. And these clues are subtle. In fact, the whole topic of nonverbal communication is filled with subtlety. That's why there are some important things to remember about its characteristics:

(teamwork)

I. Nonverbal Communication Means You're Always "Talking."

Don't forget this! We are all walking billboards, but what are we advertising?

As you walk down the hallway of your church, peeking in each room, greeting your leaders with a wave or a hug, you are communicating. Giving eye contact, shaking hands, offering a hug, or moving toward someone with a smile are all signs of favorable communication. Scripture reminds us that

Bright eyes gladden the heart. —Proverbs 15:30, NASB

I tell my staff that a smile is an inexpensive way to improve their looks. Your face is telling a story whether you like it or not. Crossed arms, glazed stares, wandering eyes that keep looking away—all indicate disinterest. The way you walk, talk, handle problems, deal with difficulty, rejoice, and have fun are signals to others of what is really going on inside.

Long periods of silence at the dinner table will communicate just as clearly as any words that could be used to describe your feelings at that moment. "Happiness makes a person smile, but sadness can break a person's spirit" (Proverbs 15:13, NCV). You can spot happiness without a word, and you can spot a broken spirit without a word. The ability to recognize these situations will make you a stronger leader and a better minister to those you serve. You may think you are only talking to yourself, but you are always communicating, from the moment another person observes you.

2. Nonverbal Communication Carries an Emotional Punch.

It puts the exclamation point on our verbal communication. Social researcher Albert Mehrabian found that only about 7 percent of the emotional meaning of a message is communicated through explicit verbal channels. About 38 percent is communicated by tone of voice. About 55 percent comes through nonverbal signals, which include such things as gestures, posture, and facial expressions.[1] Behavior other than spoken or written communication creates or represents meaning. Listening only to spoken words causes us to miss much of the speaker's meaning.

> At some level, even a child can recognize that nonverbal communication carries an emotional punch that often needs no words.

If we're excited about something, we generally become more animated. Our hands get moving, our eyes open wide, we move our body around, and we smile and convey genuine energy. If you'd just won a new car and you were telling a friend about it, how would you deliver the good news? Certainly not with a monotone voice and a blank expression on your face.

But how do you communicate to your team members, or the children in your ministry? Author and lecturer Leo Buscaglia once spoke of a contest he was asked to judge. The purpose of the contest was to find the most caring child. The winner was a four-year-old boy who had an elderly neighbor who had recently lost his wife. Upon seeing the man weeping, the little boy went into the old

PRACTICAL PATHWAY

Picking Up Those Nonverbal Clues

When you attempt to pick up *everything* that's being communicated to you, it's important to know what to look for—not just listen to—while listening. Jo-Ellan Dimitrius, a nationally known expert in "reading" people for jury selection, suggests these steps when you hope to glean some clues about what's *really* on someone's mind[2]:

Scan from head to toe:

You'll never know where you'll find that critical clue—hairstyle, watch, shoes, chewed fingernails—unless you look everywhere.

But don't judge a book—or a person—by its cover:

Our physical appearance, dress, and body language always provide clues but seldom definitive answers about our personalities and character.

Remember, it's easy to dress the part:

Characteristics which can be consciously adopted—such as hairstyle, dress, and even a distinctive walk—generally have less meaning when viewed in isolation than involuntary actions—like a nervous laugh or furtive eyes.

Look for consistent *combinations* of clues:

If you're on the right track, the signs should point in the same direction.

Remember, involuntary body language may be the only sign of "negative" emotions or traits:

We've all learned to disguise dishonesty, resentment, and other socially undesirable traits. Keep alert; their signs will often leak out only through someone's body language.

Can You Read Body Language?

Instructions: Read the four minicases below. Then match them to the four lettered feelings. At the end of this chapter, you'll find descriptions of how people give nonverbal clues to these feelings and intentions. Reading them will help you see how you've scored on this exercise!

The Options

       A. Telling a lie?

       B. Frustrated!

       C. Bored!

       D. Grieving

The Minicases

____Seven-year-old Ashley walked into the room with her eyes downcast. She moved slowly to a chair and slumped down. When her teacher asked her to get the crayons from the cupboard, she didn't seem to know how to do it.

____Fifth-grader Stephen was talking more rapidly than usual, fidgeting and looking around the room as he rambled on. He seemed nervous about something, but the sincere expression on his face set his teacher at ease. Then Stephen walked up for a hug.

____Junior high student Juanita let her eyes wander off into the distance. She sighed heavily, stretched, and crossed her arms. "If you keep picking at your fingernails like that, they'll begin to hurt," her teacher said.

____Marcus, in the fourth-grade Sunday school class, kept looking directly into his teacher's eyes, repeating what he had already said. He also seemed to be invading his teacher's space, inching still closer.

gentleman's yard, climbed onto his lap, and just sat there. When his mother asked him what he had said to the man, the little boy replied, "Nothing. I just helped him cry."[3] Perhaps at some level, even a child can recognize that nonverbal communication carries an emotional punch that often needs no words. Use it for the good in your ministry.

3. Nonverbal Communication Is "Louder."

A few weeks ago, I was listening to one of the leaders at my church when he abruptly stopped talking in midsentence. My arms were folded across the front of my chest, my eyes surfing the background just behind him. He said, "Helloooooooo...are you OK?" He was waving his hand in front of my face.

Of course I was OK. Although I had told him I would listen, my ears were engaged but my body language showed my mind was elsewhere. I was telling this man that I honestly didn't care about what he was saying. Therefore, I was using and devaluing the person in front of me.

Because nonverbal signals are the exclamation points to our communication, they truly drive home our attitude. Body position and facial expression can make a humorous point or soften a tense moment. A good speaker knows this principle well. It's not only how you *tell* the story but how you *present* the story. Therefore, when you lead your children each weekend, don't just tell the story—*live* the story! Pauses, cadence, and voice inflection all add power to your words.

Every year at Gettysburg, Pennsylvania, the Gettysburg Address is commemorated with a special public reading. I've been told that back in the 1920s a certain bishop was selected to read the speech. As the story goes, an old man shuffled up and said, "Sir, I just want you to know that you did the address wrong."

The bishop was offended and pulled out his notes, inspecting them closely. He said, "No, look, I read this correctly."

The old man said, "No, you really didn't do it right. You see, I was here when Mr. Lincoln gave that address."

"Well, how did Mr. Lincoln do it?" asked the bishop.

"You know that section in there where it says, 'the government for the people and by the people'? Well, when Mr. Lincoln got to that section, he put his hands out over the crowd, like giving a benediction. You see, when Mr. Lincoln spoke, he emphasized *people*. When you gave the Address today, you emphasized *government*."

4. Nonverbal Communication Is Much More Believable!

This is a crucial truth, an often-heard truth, but we must learn it well: "Actions speak louder than words."

In the world of nonverbal communication, these are called "cues." A cue is simply something you *do* that may or may not be backed up by what you *say*. Someone once said, "What you are doing is thundering above your head so loud I can't hear what you are saying." Let's make sure our words and actions agree.

(teamwork)

Try These Nonverbal Techniques

Now that we recognize the importance of paying attention to our nonverbal signals, let's consider what we can do to make those signals more beneficial to team unity. If you're a ministry volunteer, try these nonverbal techniques as you check children in and out of your rooms and interact with parents and other leaders. If you are a ministry leader or children's pastor, you'll find these skills useful as well:

→1. Smile, regardless of how your day is going.

THOUGHT: The most inexpensive way to communicate goodwill to others—and improve your own looks as well—is to smile.

VERSE: "Happiness makes a person smile, but sadness can break a person's spirit." —Proverbs 15:13, NCV

PRACTICAL APPLICATION: Be aware of your face this week. You have heard the expression, "Put on a happy face." We say it all the time to our kids. We say, "Let me see that smile." The initial response is "No!" But after a while, the smile comes. Bless someone this week by giving them the gift of your smile.

→2. Reach out with the appropriate touch.

THOUGHT: We send e-mails, circulate memos, make phone calls, leave voice mails, send faxes, and communicate verbally all through the day. Oddly enough, in our hurried lives, it seems we have a lot of time for communicating but no time for a handshake, a high five, or a pat on the shoulder. This concept of slowing down for a hug is relatively new to many of us. However, I have learned to "embrace" the idea of communicating authentically my love for those in ministry with me.

VERSE: "A man with leprosy came and knelt in front of Jesus, begging to be healed. 'If you want to, you can make me well again,' he said. Moved with pity, Jesus touched him. 'I want to,' he said. 'Be healed!' Instantly the leprosy disappeared—the man was healed." —Mark 1:40-42, NLT

PRACTICAL APPLICATION: Give some thought to the verse above. A person who had contracted leprosy was put out of the city to live a life of exile. Yet, interestingly enough, the word "touch" in this verse means more than a brush or handshake. It means "to fasten to" or "lay hold of." More than a handshake, it was an affectionate embrace. That's what Jesus did!

→3. Look 'em in the eye, and give the nod.

THOUGHT: Yes, maintain eye contact as you speak and listen. Some say that the eyes are the windows to the heart. I don't know whether that is true, but I know people can read your sincerity from the way you use your eyes.

VERSE: "A twinkle in the eye delights the heart. Good news refreshes the body."—Proverbs 15:30, GWT

PRACTICAL APPLICATION: Maintaining eye contact shows interest in the person you are talking to. The first time I spoke in front of a large audience, I was scared to death. I remember a guy named Jim sitting in the front row. The reason I remember him was because of the way he was responding to me during the lesson. He was writing things down, smiling, giving me eye contact, and nodding in approval. I found myself teaching to one guy out of 2,000 because of the excellent feedback he was giving me. So remember to provide responsive feedback to the person you are communicating with. A nod here and there works well.

→4. Use gestures, be animated—it's OK!

THOUGHT: Use your arms when you talk. God didn't stitch your wrists to your legs. Caution: For those of you who already do this, there is a difference between helpful gestures and flailing! (You know who you are.)

VERSE: "Never be lacking in zeal, but keep your spiritual fervor, serving the Lord." —Romans 12:11

PRACTICAL APPLICATION: If you have zeal and energy, you have just got to move! Try communicating once or twice this week *without* talking—just using your face and hands and energy. What kind of response do you receive?

→5. Slow down and smell the roses.

THOUGHT: This is to balance Number 4 above, and I have a confession to make: This is the toughest one for me, personally. I feel as if I am constantly in a rush, and I put others at odds when I am moving around them so fast. I have a tendency to be a bit *intense* (other applicable words might be "driven" or "focused"—nice words we use for people like me). The bottom line? The world will continue to spin, even if you stop pushing it.

QUOTE: James Dittes said, "[We] learn to shuffle through leaves on a golden day without wonder, or to stare at a bleak landscape or at birds in flight without longing. We learn to mute the joy we feel at special moments of rapture. We learn to disengage from life, at the

(teamwork)

gain of lessening grief, and at the cost of lessening life...We smog our vision, flatten our path, drug our sensibilities, and siphon off our energies in dull routines such as jogging...and cable T.V."[4]

PRACTICAL APPLICATION: We were debriefing an event, and my final question of the meeting was, "Is there anything else?"

One staff member said, "Craig, we really liked how calm you were during this event." It made me wonder: *Does my staff normally think I'm NOT calm?*

I try to say the right things, and I probably do, but my actions speak louder than my words when I run around like crazy. It likely hurts the performance of the rest of my team, making them tense as a kind of chain reaction.

One final word of caution: As you pay attention to the "signals" being sent your way, be careful not to fixate on a single nonverbal cue. For instance, just because a person has arms crossed in a conversation doesn't mean the person doesn't care what you're saying. It may simply mean he or she is cold. So look for *clusters* of cues. For example, arms crossed with a frown and flat tone of voice may indicate the person has an issue with you. You probably need to *listen* to what the person is *saying!*

Current research indicates there are about 125 nonverbal signals cataloged as recognizable. These nonverbal cues give our days the "look" and "feel" we remember long after words have died away.

So what are you saying today when you don't open your mouth?

For Reflection and Discussion

1. What is your expertise at communicating on the levels discussed at the beginning of this chapter? Where do you or your group need to improve?

2. When have you been "emotionally punched" by nonverbal communication? How did you respond?

3. Do you agree that nonverbal communication is more believable? Why? Can you give an example?

4. How would you evaluate yourself when it comes to practicing the five suggested nonverbal techniques? Take some time in your group to give one another feedback about your responses.

Descriptions of Nonverbal Clues

Dishonesty: shifty or wandering eyes; any type of fidgeting; rapid speech; any signs of nervousness; an exaggerated version of the "sincere, furrowed-brow look"; sweating; shaking; any activity that obscures the eyes, face, or mouth, such as putting the hand over the mouth while talking, rubbing the nose, or blinking the eyes; licking lips; running tongue over the teeth; inappropriate familiarity, such as backslapping, other touching, and getting too close

Boredom: letting eyes wander, gazing into the distance, glancing at one's watch or other objects, sighing heavily, yawning, crossing and uncrossing legs and arms, doodling, stretching, cradling one's chin in hand while glancing around the room, picking at fingernails or clothing

Frustration: frequent, direct eye contact; uttering repetitive phrases; closeness to the other person (frequently within his or her personal space); gesturing with the hands, pointing, shrugging

Grief/Sorrow: listlessness, inability to complete normal daily tasks, isolation, apathy, downcast eyes, relaxed facial muscles, slumped or slackened body, motionlessness, or slow and deliberate motion

Endnotes

1. Albert Mehrabian, *Nonverbal Communication* (Chicago: Aldine-Atherton, 1972), 43.

2. Jo-Ellan Dimitrius and Mark Mazzarella, *Reading People: How to Understand People and Predict Their Behavior— Anytime, Anyplace* (New York: Ballantine Books, 1999), 74-75.

3. Ellen Kreidman, "The Most Caring Child," *A 3rd Serving of Chicken Soup for the Soul* (Deerfield Beach, FL: Health Communications, Inc., 1996).

4. James E. Dittes, *The Male Predicament: On Being a Man Today* (San Francisco: Harper and Row, 1985), 58, quoted in Joseph Biuso and Brian Newman, *Receiving Love* (Wheaton: Victor Books, 1996), 139.

NINE

→Bronze, Silver, Gold, or Platinum?

You may have a huge roster of individuals running your ministry. You may have volunteers coming out of the woodwork. You may have two volunteers per child! But if you don't have a team, what fun is it and how effective is it? How consistent is the care given to the children? And are you really carrying out the ministry that Christ gave to the church—that together we edify one another into spiritual maturity?

Here is what I know: A group of disconnected individuals meeting once a month will not outperform a team of leaders serving side by side with one another, building relationships with one another, week in and week out. That would be like trying to win a World Series by changing the players every week. It's just not going to happen.

We need one another. In fact, have you ever considered the "one anothers" in the Bible? Here's just a short list to get you started:

→Love one another (John 13:34).

→Be devoted to one another (Romans 12:10).

→Accept one another (Romans 15:7).

→Instruct one another (Romans 15:14).

→Greet one another with affection (Romans 16:16).

→Serve one another (Galatians 5:13).

→Bear with one another in love (Ephesians 4:2).

→Be kind and compassionate to one another (Ephesians 4:32).

→Forgive one another (Ephesians 4:32).

→Wisely admonish one another (Colossians 3:16).

→Build one another up (1 Thessalonians 5:11).

→Encourage one another daily (Hebrews 3:13).

→Spur one another into doing good (Hebrews 10:24).

→Keep meeting with one another (Hebrews 10:25).

We can't do all these things if there is no "other" to do them with! God calls us to do his ministry together with sanctified teamwork that is competent and consistent. Then we will have success that we can all enjoy in serving with one another.

So let's think for a moment about team success. It's crucial to doing the will of God in children's ministry. Last time I checked, we all needed other leaders to be involved for children's ministry to work and be successful. Now I tend to overuse acronyms in my teaching, as anyone who knows me will quickly tell you (in fact, one of my staff members teased me by using an acronym of my last name: JUTILA: Just Understand These Incredibly Long Acronyms). Nevertheless, I'm going to fall into my old habits and suggest an acronym you can put into play when it comes to evaluating the health of your teams: "S-U-C-C-E-S-S-F-U-L":

S—Share a Common Vision

What is your shared vision? How do you state it? Ask yourself: Where is our children's ministry going? If you know where you're going, you'll be sharing common themes and tasks. Here at Saddleback, we're going to share Christ with the children of our community, team them with other believers, and help them advance spiritually while recognizing their spiritual gifts and surrendering their lives to God. This is our basic mission statement.

> As long as you share the vision, you can all head in the same direction.

That's where we are going with our team. You may have a different vision with your own unique goals. As long as you share the vision, you can all head in the same direction. Commit your mission statement to memory, and encourage your team members to do likewise.

U—Understate One Another's Weaknesses

A man was in the hospital recovering from a fall from his roof, and he was looking at his wife. He said, "Wanda, you've always been there, you really have. When I flunked the tenth grade, you were there. When I wrecked my dad's new car, you were there. When I got fired at the plant, you were there. When I lost all my savings on that ostrich farm, you were there. Now I've broken my arm and leg falling off the roof, and you were there. Wanda, I just want you to know that you've been nothing but bad luck to me!"

He was so close to getting it—until letting loose with the slammer at the end. What about you? When you're in a group, do you accentuate the positive or play up the negative? There are always at least two ways to look at a team member's contribution. You can choose to see it in the best light possible and downplay the weaknesses, or you can focus on what's wrong and nit-pick his or her performance. You can afford to do the former, because you're bringing together the strengths of many. In most cases, the strengths of others will make up for the weaknesses of one.

(teamwork)

C—Communicate Goals Clearly

Last week, our team reviewed notes from last year, to see whether we were meeting our goals. The overwhelming response, on a scale of 1 to 10, was a 9, for a high level of success. We found we were meeting the goals we'd set for ourselves a year ago.

But we couldn't have known of our success unless we had actually written our specific goals and objectives, with due dates for each and specific criteria for distinguishing between success and "needing improvement." When we ask people to get involved, we need to tell them exactly what it will mean for them to be effective. Then they can look back and clearly know what has been accomplished—and then have cause for rejoicing or readjusting.

C—Communicate Regularly

I had saved our notes from the previous years' staff meetings so I could review them during the current year. From the beginning, I had planned to ask: "Where are we?" But I didn't do it that way. I didn't wait a year to ask the question. Instead, I asked the question virtually every week; we regularly talked about our progress as an ongoing dialogue. The conversation took place between me and my staff, and also among the staff members and between the staff and their volunteers. In this way, we were training everyone to think in terms of specifics: specific goals, criteria, accomplishments, and prayers of thankfulness for the things accomplished.

> Remember, if you don't know where you are going, then any road will get you there.

We have to be able to measure where we're going. Where have you come in the last year with the kids in your class? Where have you been with ministry enrichment? Where are you when it comes to encouraging leaders above you and those who are trying to serve you? Are you all communicating regularly? Remember, if you don't know where you are going, then any road will get you there.

E—Evaluate and Adjust

The good teams evaluate and make adjustments as needed. I played college baseball with a teammate who was a unique hitter. Even though he was a right-handed batter, he would always, always hit the ball to the right side of the field, between first and second base.

During one game in our senior year, I recall that when he came up to bat, every player on the opposing team shifted to the right side of the field to defend against what they knew would happen should this guy make contact. The left fielder, the short stop, the third baseman—all moved to the right side of second base. It was a strange sight: All the way to the outfield, from center field to left field, was a vacant lot of nice, green grass just begging my friend to drop a fly ball. It would roll and roll and roll. It was an inside-the-park homer just waiting to happen. All he had to do was hit the ball to the left side.

He couldn't do it. He went 0-4 that day. Why? Because the other team evaluated its previous efforts (and the efforts of other teams we'd played) and realized they had a better chance of getting him out by moving everybody over. And they were successful all four times that day.

As a team, we need to evaluate. And when we read "the writing on the wall," we need the courage to make the necessary adjustments.

S—Share a Common Direction

Typically, people who share a common direction get where they're going more quickly. The flight habits of geese wonderfully illustrate this point. It's aerodynamically better for them to fly in a V formation because, as each bird flaps its wings, it creates an uplift for the bird following immediately behind it. It's been deduced that by using this flying formation, the entire flock has 71 percent greater lift. Who are we providing a lift for today by moving in a common direction?

Here's another interesting and helpful aspect about "goose goodwill" that we can apply to our own teams: Geese share leadership, so the lead goose doesn't always fly in front, having to brave the full force of the air friction. Rather, after the leader gets tired of bearing the brunt of everything, he slips to the back. When everyone shares a common direction, good leadership will do that and just let the team begin to carry the load. The team is responsible, not just one person.

S—Show Loyalty

Two men riding a tandem bike came to a steep hill. They started up, and it proved to be a very steep climb. When they finally reached the top, the guy in front said to the other, "Man! That was tough. What a hard climb!"

The other guy said, "Yeah, it was. If I hadn't kept the brakes on all the way, we'd have rolled down backward!"

You can look around at your team members and wonder: Who keeps putting the brakes on around here? Those folks need to say, "I'm going to show loyalty to the vision, to the direction, to the leader, and to my team members. I'm going to take my foot off the brake and surrender my individual agenda to the team agenda."

We can help team members let go of the brakes by constantly reminding ourselves of the principle that flows from Romans 12:10. It calls us to love one another like brothers and sisters, and honor one another above ourselves. Think about how important that can be to any team: At the beginning of the 1997 football season, there were 1,487 players in the NFL. Forty-four of the players were from Penn State and thirty-seven were from Notre Dame—5 percent of the NFL from those two schools alone! I find it interesting that these are the two colleges that don't put players' names on the backs of their football jerseys. The individuals have submitted themselves to the good of the team. That is loyalty.

F—Focus on the Lord

Jesus said, "My sheep follow me." There is an understanding that we have a path to follow. We're not making our own rules; we have a standard to live by. Jesus has established the standard. We have to focus on the Lord.

(teamwork)

This simply means making time during your day for pausing, lifting your heart in awareness of Christ's abiding presence with you. How often we forget that the ministry is *his* ministry. The kids are *his* kids. Our talents and skills are gifts of *his* that he has loaned us while we're here on earth. Stay aware as you work. Focus on him.

U—Unite With a Natural Fit

Some researchers tried to figure out what it would take to put a group of men together who would work for days upon days in the tight quarters of a submarine without building destructive levels of tension or succumbing to significant conflict. In other words, what would it take to put a crew together that would be able to keep "getting along" under constant strenuous conditions?

> When a person is causing you "fits," you're probably dealing with a mismatch in the chemistry between the two of you.

A Dr. Shetz headed up the research, eventually submitting a very hefty report—which all boiled down to a single sentence: You need to find a group of men who have a natural fit.

Do you ever want to say, "Well, no duh!"?

But it does remind us that chemistry can and does develop. There is kind of a chemistry that develops among individuals who bond and solidify the team. Generally speaking, when a person is causing you "fits," you're probably dealing with a mismatch in the chemistry between the two of you.[1]

It's not always possible to work with people who just seem to "fit" with us. But when it is possible, good teams try to make those matches work for them. An article in Harvard Business Review said: "Transforming a good company into a great one...include[s] getting the right people on the bus (and the wrong people off the bus)."[2] In other words, build team chemistry.

L—Listen to One Another

The biggest obstacle in personal communication is not the inability to say what's on our mind; it's the inability to listen as the other person says what's on his or her mind. Many of us are distracted by what we hope to say next. It's true, isn't it? So often, as someone speaks to me, I'm processing my response rather than listening to the speaker. Yet Proverbs 18:13 says, "He who answers before listening, that is his folly and his shame."

A couple of years ago, we were holding a conference in Canada. After one of the sessions, I talked to a few people and then began to walk out of the church. A young lady who looked as if she were just out of college, full of energy, stood in front of me with her pen ready and notebook opened. She asked me a question that took me off guard: "What makes you successful?"

Now I have to be honest, I have never thought of myself as being particularly successful. I have, however, thought of our team as successful. So I thought for a moment and gave my answer: "It's my ability to gather people around me who are smarter than I am."

I am an ordinary, weak individual. God was doing fine before me, and he is going to be doing great when I am gone. There is no room for an arrogant individual on a team. But there's lots of room on your team for people who know more—and can do things better—than you. Will you gather them? Will your self-esteem allow for them?

Do You Have a Competent Team?

You want to pull together people who will produce a competent team. A few years ago, I was putting together a church hockey team that was going to play at a new rink opening up in our city. While I was at the rink filling out some paperwork and delivering our deposit, the gentleman working the counter asked me a few questions:

"Is your team bronze, silver, gold, or platinum?"

Odd question, I thought. So I said, "Huh?"

Again he asked, "Is your team bronze, silver, gold, or platinum?"

I didn't understand the question, so he explained. "See, the bronze would be a beginner level and platinum would be a tournament-cup team level." He wanted to know what the skill level of our team was. I asked him if there was a plastic league...

To make a long story short, we ended up in the bronze league and had a great time. Over the next few years, though, we found ourselves moving up in the league because the skill level of each player got better over time. As a result of each player getting better, our team, as a whole, got better.

When we form teams at our church, I find that we ask all types of "commitment" questions, "getting to know you" questions, and "how long have you been a believer" questions. These are all great questions, don't get me wrong, but if you want to play at the platinum level, you have to ask the skill question.

Assess Your Skill Level

That day when the guy at the hockey rink asked me the skill-level question, lots of things started to flow through my head. I didn't want to start at the bronze level; I wanted to be more competitive. I wanted to start at the higher level. But I had to ask myself: What, in reality, is the talent level of the people on my team? This is a competency question. It's a question for all of us in children's ministry to ponder. What is the competency level of your team?

So let me ask you, what league do you want to play in? When it comes to sharing Christ and growing kids spiritually, where are you with your team? bronze, silver, gold, or platinum? You may say, "Craig, our children's ministry isn't a competition." Well, I guess I would have to disagree. I believe we are all in a competition. Not with one another or with other churches, but we are in competition with every other use of time that a child or an adult leader has in this world. Are they getting our best?

Sure, we started at the bronze level, and over time, as skills were enhanced, the commitment on the team grew. We put some wins under our belt and gained some momentum as things began to change. We stopped playing at the bronze level, and we moved up.

In ministry, I spent many years operating at the bronze level. My own skill level was not what it should have been, nor was my commitment. There was no momentum

(teamwork)

in the early years and rarely a win—just a lot of hard work. Then, slowly, I began to work on my skills of communication, of talking to parents, of talking to kids, and I seriously studied the leadership-related issues of walking with people and building into them. Then we started adding players, key players to our ministry team, who had some skills in upfront group communication, good interpersonal skills, people who had heart and passion for kids and leadership.

And together we grew. We put some wins under our belt. And over time, as skills increased, we gained some momentum. With momentum comes confidence, a solid faith in your individual performance and faith in the team around you.

But no one can build a successful team overnight. Sure, you can throw a group of skilled players onto a basketball court, baseball field, or hockey rink, but skill alone doesn't make a team successful; it takes time. You need to have competency, chemistry, commitment, and consistency on your team. You will have to be a good leader, one who never stops learning, to see these things happen over the years.

Be a Skillful Captain

If you're a ministry leader, then aspire to lead the team with excellence. In hockey, one individual wears a C on his jersey. It stands for "Captain." Wearing the C isn't for everyone, of course. In sports, captains have tremendous responsibility. They are the first to talk with the media. They have to rally the team and keep it unified. Captains have to help players and the coaching staff work through issues and difficulties. They have to see the big picture. "Lot's of guys can see the small picture—their own situation," says Dave King, NHL coach from Columbus. "A captain has to see the bigger picture, where the entire team is going."

"You have to take care of a wider range of duties," says professional hockey player and captain, Tony Amonte. "You have to try and eliminate distractions. You want to help everyone get into the game with a clear mind."[3]

Let me push the hockey parallel to the limits as we round out this chapter. Consider:

→ Those who play, rotate lines every few minutes to take a break, catch a breath. They have balance and margin in their lives. Do you? Do you keep yourself refreshed and renewed for your tasks in children's ministry, making time on your calendar for retreats, workshops, vacations—and the occasional nap?

→ There is only one timeout allowed in hockey. You'd better be intentional when you use it! Do you ever call a timeout with your team to pause, to strategize, to let team members catch their breath and renew their vision, or to write out some plays and initiatives and goals for the year?

→ If the score is tied, the most skilled line skates more often. In any group, even in the church, there will be people who watch things happen, people who make things happen, and people who don't know what happened. When crunch time comes, you want to go with the people who make things happen in your ministry. They are usually people who have more skill and awareness. Focus on mentoring them to the fullest.

PRACTICAL PATHWAY

A Team Process for Problem Solving

Enjoying good teamwork doesn't mean that everything always runs smoothly in your team. When problems arise, a platinum-level team has a process in place for developing solutions. Here's how a problem-solving process could look, step by step.

Step 1

Survey. Circulate a survey periodically (or when conflicts seem to increase), using a very simple form. Here is an example.

Group Check
Anonymous Questionnaire

The top three STRENGTHS of this group are...

➜ _____

➜ _____

➜ _____

The top three WEAKNESSES of this group are...

➜ _____

➜ _____

➜ _____

What I NEED most from this group is...

_____

_____

_____

_____

Step 2

Distribute. Compile *all* survey responses and distribute them to *all* members at a future meeting.

Step 3

Select and prioritize. Ask for feedback about the items listed in the survey, and begin working on selecting what appear to be the most significant items (you may wish to use triads or small groups here). You'll begin forming a consensus about which selected items suggest the most pressing problem areas that need solutions.

Step 4

Clarify. Ask questions and gather information. Do we know everything we need to know about these problems or concerns? If we need more information, how will we gather it? Who will be responsible for reporting back to the group, if necessary?

Be sure everyone understands the nature of the problems you'll be tackling. Allow for some in-depth study, if needed, to clearly define causes, effects, and potential results of any actions you might take.

Step 5

Propose tentative solutions. Brainstorm and record: What are some *possible* solutions that might work? Keep the floor open for any and all suggestions. Censor no idea at this point!

Step 6

Identify the best solutions. Take the results of your brainstorming and, together, choose what appear to be the best ideas. Work at refining them—eventually attaching personnel, resources, objectives, goals, and due dates to each task.

Step 7

Implement. Now take action on your decisions! Determine a reasonable schedule and plan for Step 8.

Step 8

Evaluate and resurvey. Ask tough questions about the effectiveness of your plans. Thoroughly discuss: How is our idea working (or how did things work out)? Plan to adjust your focus and/or efforts as needed. Then start the entire cyclical process again, as appropriate.

I believe that recruiting people into children's ministry is not as important as retaining those who are already serving with us—and discipling them into "builders." If every year your "talent" is rotating off your team, you are in trouble. You will never build chemistry, which will never lead to wins, which will never lead to momentum, which will doom your ministry to mediocrity. You'll stay in the bronze league.

Likewise, if you have leaders and volunteers who are only serving once a month at your weekend service, or every other month at your weekend service, or once a year at your weekend service, you'll be so busy managing the flock that you will not shepherd the sheep! You'll be the manager of the team, not the leader of the team. You'll be filling spots, not building lives.

So, where are you today? bronze, silver, gold, or platinum? No matter where you are, I encourage you to build, invest, instill, and initiate growth opportunities so that a year from now you can look back and say, "Yes, without a doubt, as a team, we have moved up in the league."

For Reflection and Discussion

1. What letter in the SUCCESSFUL acrostic does your team need the most help with? List a few steps you will take to grow deeper in this area.

2. What is the greatest strength of your team? How will you celebrate it?

3. Is there anyone you need to add to the "bus" during the coming year? Is there anyone you need to excuse from the bus this year?

4. When it comes to practicing the biblical "one anothers," how does your church or team rate (on a scale of I to 10, with I being "terrible" and 10 being "fantastic")?

5. What is your group's common vision? How clearly can everyone articulate it? (Check it out in your team.)

6. Is your team at the bronze, silver, gold, or platinum level? What exactly does this mean to you? What will it take for you to move up in the league?

Endnotes

1. Concepts gleaned from listening to Les Parrot at a Leadership Summit at Willow Creek Church in 1998.

2. Jim Collins, "Level 5 Leadership," Harvard Business Review, January 2001, 68.

3. "History of Captains," Rinkside Magazine, December 2000, 75.

HONOR

"*be devoted to one another in brotherly love. Honor one another above yourselves.*"

—Romans 12:10

TEN

→Check Those Price Tags!

A few Christmases ago, my wife wanted a sweater—you know, one of those red-and-green numbers with the little white reindeer and snowflakes? So I headed down to the mall (with a few thousand other guys; it was December 24 and getting late in the day).

I came across a sweater, but it was displayed on a mannequin dressed for the ski lodge. I walked up and fished around on the plastic lady for the price tag and pulled out a little card that read—$250! I stepped back and thought, *Unbelievable! For a pair of slacks, a blouse, and a sweater? I could buy about nine whole cases of duct tape with money like that, or a dozen rounds of golf or—think of the pizza! Not to mention the kids' college someday. I mean, this is close to a full semester, at least, of Intro to Biology, right?*

Anyway, my visions of financial ruin were interrupted by a pleasant-looking saleswoman who floated toward me. I showed her the tag and blurted, "Wow! I was looking at this sweater, and it must be around $100 or so, based on the price of the total outfit."

Adjusting her glasses, she said, "Let me check. No, the sweater is $250."

"But what else do you get *with* the sweater?"

She looked again and said, "Actually, sir, the sweater is $250, the pants are $100, the blouse is $80, and the shoes are another $120."

There's like a couple thousand dollars hanging on this dummy!

After a few painful moments of indecision, I decided to look at it a little differently. I began to look at that sweater in a completely different way. I didn't buy it, but when I found out the value, I sure appreciated it more. When I saw the value, I even treated it differently. Why? Because of the value that was assigned to it by its creator.

The Bible tells us, "Be devoted to one another in brotherly love. Honor one another above yourselves" (Romans 12:10).

If you were studying biblical Greek 101, you'd be able to tell your friends that the original root word for "honor" is *tumei*. It carries the idea of a "price tag." In this chapter, we're going to consider how we can view others as having higher price tags—that is, value them, honor them, extend *tumei* to them, even to those persons who may have wronged us or spoken harshly to our face (or behind our back). We can honor them by seeing the price tag on their souls.

Every person you'll meet today displays that kind of price tag. Can you see it? Do you have the heart for honoring?

Experiencing Heart Trouble?

I know, sometimes it's hard to see the value in others. I suggest that our hearts often get in the way. After all, honoring is, first and foremost, a *decision*, a choice of the heart. And our hearts can block it.

> After all, honoring is, first and foremost, a *decision*, a choice of the heart.

Why do we sometimes choose to dishonor or disrespect people? I've come up with seven cardiac crises that would certainly be medically scary; as it is, they're absolutely devastating to ministry relationships.

I. The Enlarged Heart

Have you ever known someone who had "a big head"? That's the idea here—we're talking about pride. We're number one, the world revolves around us, and we see everyone as trailing along in second place. I'm making this blatant, but it can be as subtle as those feathers of frost decorating your window on a crisp winter morning. You know how subtle it can be in your own soul.

For example, maybe this Christian brother or sister standing before you doesn't have the top-caliber job you do; therefore, you look down from the heights. Maybe he doesn't have the classy coupe you have; therefore, he's in a different class. Maybe she's only a high school graduate, and you've taken honors courses in the Ivy League; therefore, you overexplain—or just ignore the opportunity to talk. It's interesting that in Matthew 20:25-27, Jesus called all the followers together and said, "You know that in this world kings are tyrants, and officials lord it over the people beneath them. But among you it should be quite different. Whoever wants to be a leader among you must be your servant, and whoever wants to be first must become your slave" (NLT).

That's the idea when you intend to treat others the way you yourself would want to be treated. To be first in God's kingdom, we need to be last. That's what we call having a second-place heart. It's not so big, but it does the job much better.

2. The High-Pressure Heart

It's ready to blow a valve or pop a vessel because of long-term stress. Look out!

In other words, do you have hypertension—emotionally or spiritually? Perhaps the stresses of life have outpaced your judgment, and you begin regularly dishonoring folks with unkind words or cutting nonverbal responses. Maybe you're in traffic, and you're going to go home and step into a family situation or a roommate situation, and you'll be "going volcano"—as usual—as soon as you walk in the door.

Beware! There will be significant hemorrhaging before too long. It took years to get this way, and the healing curve may be steep.

Of course, you end up having to go back and apologize, time and again. When our hearts succumb to the ongoing pressure, we need to be able to say, "Let's pace through this; let's begin to deal with things together." We cannot let the pressures—even the routines of our lives—outpace our judgment. We need to cultivate hearts of peace rather than vent upon those waiting for us with hopeful expectancy in their own hearts.

3. The Shoved-Back Heart

This sounds like a weird physical phenomenon, and it would certainly be serious as a bodily ailment. Sadly, it's just as serious when it's a spiritual issue. It's similar to the high-pressure heart, except this disease hits in one big burst rather than developing over time.

You're feeling as if you've just been shoved. For example, you're on vacation, the airline has lost your luggage, so *you have a right* to get that luggage back, ASAP. Or maybe you're at a restaurant, and it's a little expensive, but you don't feel as if you've received the service that *you have a right* to enjoy. The waiter is in a bad mood, so he's shoving you back.

I think of the train conductor who was out of control, dishonoring people all along the way. He came to a man in the back who had the wrong ticket and cut loose on him.

But the man apologized to the conductor and treated the conductor with honor, even though this passenger had just been brutalized by a verbal barrage. When the conductor moved on to the next car, a man sitting across from the guy who apologized said, "Wow! I can't believe how you responded! Giving him such respect when he was being so rotten!"

"Hey, that guy has to live with himself all year," the man said. "I can put up with him for five minutes."

That's the way we have to look at it. Hurt people have a tendency to hurt people. We have to figure out where they're coming from, so that even if we feel as if they've shoved back our heart, we can see through God's eyes and love them anyway.

4. The Drained Heart

Imagine your heart being drained of blood—not good. But imagine if your heart were drained of spirit—or the Holy Spirit! Definitely not good.

Not taking a daily time to walk with God? Not doing the things that keep you growing in Christ? Then your heart is draining. The Bible says,

How can you who are evil say anything good? For out of the overflow of the heart the mouth speaks. The good man brings good things out of the good stored up in him, and the evil man brings evil things out of the evil stored up in him.
—Matthew 12:34-35

We really speak from what's inside. The question is, Are you having a daily quiet time? Are you having a prayer time so the inside is clean?

I've been told that when Berlin was still divided, the communist East Berliners couldn't travel into the free side. But on one anger-filled night, some people in East Berlin got together some garbage, loaded it in a dump truck, and snuck across into West Berlin and dumped the mess all over the streets. They fled back home on foot.

> We have to make sure our hearts aren't spiritually drained, because each of us gives out of what we have available in our giving store-house.

The next day, they wanted to see what the reaction would be from West Berlin. Nothing. Except that the next day, some townspeople in the West got together, cleaned out the truck, and filled it with canned goods, clothes, water, lots of nice things. They snuck across into East Berlin that night and left the truck on a street. They put a sign next to it, though. The sign read, "Each gives out of what each has to give."

That's not bad. We have to make sure our hearts aren't spiritually drained, because each of us gives out of what we have available in our giving storehouse.

5. The Murmuring Heart

Some folks have a heart murmur, and they live with it all of their lives. Others of us have murmuring hearts; if we have to live with *that*, day in and day out, we end up making ourselves miserable. And we infect others with our constant complaining. The murmuring heart might make strange noises like these:

→ "He owes me." (Therefore, I'll give him nothing until I get what I need for myself.)

→ "They've treated me badly for years." (Thus, I will dishonor them until their attitudes change.)

→ "I do all the work around here." (So, I'll just keep doing it with a bad attitude.)

→ "She never gives me any praise." (Hey, do you really think I'm going to compliment *her*?)

One of the biggest relationship-ruining murmurs sounds like this under the stethoscope: "I'll never forgive her for what she did." Of course, the Bible doesn't allow us to hold people in the limbo land of unforgiveness. No, we're supposed to take action, instead. Recall these instructive words about the very first step to take:

If a believer does something wrong, go, confront him when the two of you are alone. If he listens to you, you have won back that believer. —Matthew 18:15, GWT

In Matthew 18:21–22, we gain more insight: "Then Peter came to Jesus and asked him, 'Lord, how often do I have to forgive a believer who wrongs me? Seven times?' Jesus answered him, 'I tell you, not just seven times, but seventy times seven'" (GWT).

Take a little time out right now to consider your own levels of forgiveness. Here is a quotation to meditate upon the next time your heart begins to murmur about the hurts you've had to endure from somebody who just won't seem to change. Remember that holding a grudge is a way to really hurt...*yourself.*

*"You will know that forgiveness has begun **when you recall those who hurt you and feel the power to wish them well."**[1]*

6. The Slow-Beating Heart

This is the "I'll get around to it when I get a chance" heart. It plagues the person who is slow to offer affirmation and recognition when and where it is due.

I always say that "we need the courage to say the last 10 percent." You see, we're more than willing to critique peoples' efforts by providing the first 90 percent of our observations about their work. We gladly tell them where they've failed, where they could improve, where we'd like them to be next year, and so on. This is needed, of course, especially if we're mentoring them in ministry. However, why do we stop short of stating the *good* we've seen? All the improvement, the effort, the successes—as small as they may be—seem to float away and hardly show up on our affirmation radar.

Some of that last 10 percent is very difficult to acknowledge, because the accomplishment is hardly at the level we ourselves might achieve. It's positive, perhaps, but not entirely satisfactory. So we hold back the 10 percent.

Maybe you need to go to a co-teacher or leader, maybe someone in the ministry, even one of the kids, and say, "I'm not going to be satisfied anymore with a slow delivery on the affirmation around here. I'm going to say the last 10 percent. In fact, I'm going to say that before I say anything else. And if I don't get around to the rest, at least for now, then that's OK. I really value you and honor you; what a great job you're doing!" We just need to say it more, because that honor, if given to one another, will increase the ministry momentum across the board.

7. The Atrophied Heart

Now we've come full circle from the "enlarged heart." This is the heart that is too small. It can only reach out to the familiar and the comfortable, to those who are liked and nonthreatening, to the attractive and helpful. This is a sad condition that causes a person to shrink away from all the potential warmth and love that could be available in a mature interpersonal relationship.

In his book *And the Angels Were Silent*[2] Max Lucado tells a story about a young man from Florida, John Blanchard, who had gone to the library to read a book. Instead, he became more interested in the notes penciled in the margins by the book's original owner, a woman named Miss Hollis Maynell. He was intrigued by the thoughtful reflections in the jottings and decided he would try to locate her, even though, on the very next day, he would be shipped overseas for service in World War II. He discovered that Hollis lived in New York City, so he wrote a letter of introduction and started a correspondence with her that lasted for more than a year while he was in Europe.

A romance began to develop, and John requested a photograph. Hollis refused, saying that if he really cared for her, it wouldn't matter what she looked like. When the day finally came for him to return from Europe, they scheduled their first meeting— 7:00 p.m. at Grand Central Station in New York. "You'll recognize me," she wrote, "by the red rose I'll be wearing on my lapel."

So at 7:00, John was in the station looking for a girl whose heart he loved, but whose face he'd never seen. Here is how Max Lucado tells the rest of the story from John's perspective:

A young woman was coming toward me, her figure long and slim. Her blonde hair lay back in curls from her delicate ears; her eyes were blue as flowers. Her lips and chin had a gentle firmness, and in her pale green suit she was like springtime come alive. I started toward her, entirely forgetting to notice that she was not wearing a rose.

As I moved, a small, provocative smile curved her lips. "Going my way, sailor?" she murmured. Almost uncontrollably I made one step closer to her, and then I saw Hollis Maynell. She was standing almost directly behind the girl. A woman well past forty, she had graying hair tucked under a worn hat. She was more than plump, her thick-ankled feet thrust into low-heeled shoes.

The girl in the green suit was walking quickly away. I felt as though I was split in two, so keen was my desire to follow her, and yet so deep was my longing for the woman whose spirit had truly companioned me and upheld my own. And there she stood. Her pale, plump face was gentle and sensible, her gray eyes had a warm and kindly twinkle. I did not hesitate. My fingers gripped the small worn blue leather copy of the book that was to identify me to her.

This would not be love, but it would be something precious, something perhaps even better than love, a friendship for which I had been and must ever be grateful.

I squared my shoulders and saluted and held out the book to the woman, even though while I spoke I felt choked by the bitterness of my disappointment. "I'm Lieutenant John Blanchard, and you must be Miss Maynell. I am so glad you could meet me; may I take you to dinner?"

The woman's face broadened into a tolerant smile. "I don't know what this is about, son," she answered, "but the young lady in the green suit who just went by, she begged me to wear this rose on my coat. And she said if you were to ask me out to dinner, I should go and tell you that she is waiting for you in the big restaurant across the street. She said it was some kind of test!"

It is not difficult to understand and admire Miss Maynell's wisdom, says Max Lucado. The true nature of a heart is seen in the response to the unattractive. "Tell me who you *love*," one philosopher wrote, "and I will tell you who you *are*."

PRACTICAL PATHWAY

Is Your God Image Accurate?

It's been said that the essence of idolatry is the entertainment of thoughts about God that are unworthy of him. Do you agree?

The fact is, our ability to value others hinges greatly upon our ability to value ourselves before God. There is a kind of chain reaction here: Our God image largely determines our own self-image (because, for instance, if we view God as loving, then we are loved; on the other hand, if God is understood as primarily judging and vindictive, then we constantly exist in a mode of guilt and fear). Our own self-image significantly influences our "image" of others—that is, how free we are to see the value in them. A distorted image can begin early in life, especially if you grew up with parents who were abusive or distant.

So it's critical to assess your God image. Is it accurate?

Many years ago, Bible scholar J. B. Phillips wrote a book titled *Your God Is Too Small*,[3] in which he spoke of some of the typical "distorted" God images that people have developed. If you find your God anywhere on the list below (adapted from Phillips' list) then begin a corrective process. You might begin by reading and meditating upon the scriptural descriptions of the true God during your quiet times in the coming year.

The "Unreal" Gods

→Resident policeman: our conscience

→Parental hangover: God as the image of our earthly father

→Grand old man: old-fashioned and naive

→Meek and mild: God as "Baby Jesus," soft and sentimental

→Absolute perfection: demanding 100 percent; unbending

→Heavenly bosom: a comforting escape

→God-in-a-box: obviously a Baptist, Lutheran, Methodist...

→Managing director: controlling the cosmos; uninterested in our "little" problems

→Secondhand God: based on book and film portrayals of "life"

→Perennial grievance: doesn't fulfill our expectations and plans

→Pale Galilean: a negative, no fun killjoy

The True God (just to get you started)

→ Loving (Matthew 10:28-31; Romans 8:31-39; 1 John 3:1-3)

→ Trustworthy (Exodus 15:26; Numbers 23:19)

→ Faithful (Hebrews 10:23, 35-37)

→ Giving (1 John 5:14-15)

→ Protective (Psalm 27:1-5; Psalm 91:1-7; Isaiah 43:2)

→ Gracious (Nehemiah 9:17; Ephesians 1:7-8)

→ Kind (Psalm 86:15; Psalm 119:156)

→ Merciful (Genesis 18:16-33; Ephesians 2:1-5)

→ Hates sin (Isaiah 9:17)

The God I Discover Through Personal Bible Study

Can You Start Valuing—the Way God Does?

The price tag is everything when it comes to honor. *And you determine the price tag that you want to see.*

This means you need to be aware of the value you're placing on every individual in your world. It makes all the difference in how you treat people, how they treat you, and eventually, how effectively the work of the kingdom is accomplished. In other words, the issue of the price tag determines your ministry success!

This came home to me so powerfully during an event that, on the face of it, would seem to have very little significance. My wife and I were invited to some friends' house for dinner a few years ago. Their son had a huge baseball card collection, and as soon as we got settled in the living room, he came downstairs from his bedroom and handed me some of his cards, along with a little book, the *Beckett* price guide.

I was trying to talk to his dad, but the boy kept coming down with cards, one after another. "This one's worth one dollar," he'd say. Or looking in his *Beckett*, he'd announce, "These are worth ten bucks."

He had my attention. I began looking at the *Beckett* guide myself. His dad told him to run up and get a couple of his cards from when he (Dad) was a kid. So he did. The cards were encased in five-inch blocks of plastic, with screws in the corners, to keep the cards in perfect condition. We looked up these cards, and the first one was worth $1,500.

Now I was getting truly excited and thinking about the cards I still had from when I was a kid. So we started bringing more cards downstairs. This one was worth $100; that one was valued at $200. When all was said and done, my first year's salary as a children's pastor was sitting on the table.

My wife was calmly talking to the other wife, but my mind was going a hundred miles an hour. I was thinking, *I have baseball cards at my house where I grew up! All those cards from my childhood are surely still there, up in the attic. Just lying there in shoe boxes, just waiting to be sold, just waiting to make me a small fortune.*

Then the horror struck me. Mom had called me last week. She mentioned that she was cleaning out my old room...she mentioned something about...*baseball cards.* Something about, "What did I want her to do with them?"

What had I told her? "Throw them away." (Can you feel my pain?)

We sat down for dinner, but I couldn't even think about eating and could hardly hold a conversation. I was watching the clock: 9:00, 10:00, 11:00, 12:00. My stomach was churning. While we had dessert, I was thinking, *I have to get to my mom's house* right now.

We left our friends' house about 1:00 a.m. In the car, Mary kicked off her shoes and said, "I'm exhausted. Great night. Let's go home and get a good night's sleep."

My response? "We are *not* going home! We're going over to Mom's house right now, and we're going to find those cards!" I was praying that my mom had kept them.

Mom wasn't home; she was out of the country. I didn't have a key, so I broke into the house and headed into my old room looking for these cards.

At first, they were nowhere to be found. *Mom actually threw them away!*

Finally, I went through a couple of shelves of stuff, and I found them at the back of a shelf. I was so excited! Mom had organized them all, so I took those under my arm.

As soon as I woke up the next morning, I headed right over to the bookstore to pick up my *Beckett* price guide. I came back home and spread thousands of cards all over the floor.

I discovered that one of my cards was worth $250—my 1975 George Brett rookie card. I thought that was incredible! Then I remembered that my friend had his cards encased in plastic. So I went out and got plastic cases for my cards so nothing could damage them. I was really valuing these cards.

Of course, I had some other cards, "common cards" they're called. They are only worth about a dime or so. But the ones with value—they went into the plastic cases, into nice boxes, and I treated them differently—the royal treatment for those cards.

When my wife walked in, she asked, "What's all this?" I put my finger to my mouth and said, "Shh. Look at all of these cards. These cards over here on the table are all the valuable cards I have. I've added them up, and the value is about $2,000."

Mary said, "We're rich!"

I said, "What do you mean *we*?"

Value the People, Too!

I was very excited to see the value of some of these cards that I'd collected earlier. Decidedly, I made some choices on how I treated some cards versus the other cards. And I want to draw three applications about the role of people value when it comes to honoring them.

1. Our Worth Is Decided by God in His Word.

Just as the card value is decided by Mr. Beckett's book, our worth is decided by God's book. The Bible tells us in Psalm 139:14, "I praise you because I am fearfully and wonderfully made; your works are wonderful. I know that full well." God values us before we can perform in the least. Our worth is *decided* by God in his Word, not attributed to us based on our actions. Our calling is to see ourselves through God's eyes, not how other people see us, not based on what we've accomplished in life, but based on how God sees us. That's extremely valuable.

My wife came in one day and said, "Honey, don't be mad, OK?"

"OK. What happened?"

"I was pulling out of the garage, and I hit your car."

I had a choice at that point. I could choose to honor a thing, a car, over my wife. Or I could honor my wife over a car. Was I disappointed? Yeah. Does it need to be fixed? Yeah. But cars can be fixed or replaced. I said, "OK."

2. We Need to See Others as God Sees Us.

Philippians 2:3 says, "Do nothing out of selfish ambition or vain conceit, but in humility consider others better than yourselves." When we see others through God's eyes, we begin to see how valuable they are. Remember, our choice to honor others is not based on whether or not they deserve it; it's based on their value as beings created in God's image. When we see others as God sees them, we start to *treat* others as God treats them, too.

3. If We Perceive Something as Valuable, We'll Do Anything to Find It.

Remember my frantic search for the baseball cards? Maybe there's a situation in your life that already has potential conflict written on it—maybe it's with a parent, a friend, or a co-worker. If that relationship is valuable to you (and it should be), then you need to find the person you're thinking of right now and heal that relationship. Consider Luke 15:3-7:

> **Jesus spoke to them using this illustration: "Suppose a man has 100 sheep and loses one of them. Doesn't he leave the 99 sheep grazing in the pasture and look for the lost sheep until he finds it? When he finds it, he's happy. He puts that sheep on his shoulders and goes home. Then he calls his friends and neighbors together and says to them, 'Let's celebrate! I've found my lost sheep!' I can guarantee that there will be more happiness in heaven over one person who turns to God and changes the way he thinks and acts than over 99 people who already have turned to God and have his approval." —GWT**

> *If we perceive something as valuable, we need to find it and heal it and begin to show it honor.*

If we perceive something as valuable, we need to find it and heal it and begin to show it honor. Go ahead, strive to restore relationships that have been hurt in your past.

Even When It Hurts

Decades ago, King George spoke at the opening session of the London Arms Conference. But Americans almost missed that speech because just moments before the king's voice was to go out across the airwaves in America, a control-room operator at CBS tripped over the wire and broke it. Just seconds before the king's address, Harold Videan, who was the chief control operator in those days, stepped forward. With one hand he took an end of the broken wire and with the other hand he took the other end of the broken wire—and 250 volts of electricity traveled through his arms and coursed through his body. But the king's message went out to the people. (Videan was unharmed because of the closed circuit. But would you take that risk?)[4]

If we're to be a channel of our King's message, we had best hold on very tightly, because sometimes it's going to hurt. Sometimes those we choose to respect continue to treat us with disrespect. God says to respect them anyway. Sometimes that hurts. Sometimes those we choose to love continue to treat us with unlovely actions. God says to love them anyway. That hurts. Sometimes those we choose to honor continue to treat us with dishonor. God says to honor them anyway. Sometimes that hurts.

So the question is, Are we going to allow God's message to flow through us, even when it hurts? That's what it's all about. Value and honor your neighbor as yourself.

For Reflection and Discussion

1. Have you ever had the experience of someone undervaluing you? How did you react?

2. Of all the heart conditions listed in this chapter, which is most likely to attack you personally? Why? When confronted with dishonor, how does your heart respond these days?

3. Is there anyone you perceive as valuable who is "lost" right now? Pick up the phone or start an e-mail to that person! Do whatever it takes to find him or her.

4. How do you "renew" when you are spiritually drained? What do you need to do during the coming month to refresh your spiritual life?

5. How did the story of John Blanchard affect you? What ministry applications can you draw?

Endnotes

1. Lewis B. Smedes, *Forgive and Forget* (New York: Simon and Schuster, Inc., 1984), 47.

2. Max Lucado, *And the Angels Were Silent* (Sisters, OR: Multnomah Books, 1992).

3. J. B. Phillips, *Your God Is Too Small* (New York: Macmillan, 1971), 5.

4. Donald W. McCullough, *The Trivialization of God: The Dangerous Illusion of a Manageable Deity* (Colorado Springs, CO: NavPress), 127.

ELEVEN

→Sailing the Seas of Conflict— Without Getting Sunk

The great Admiral George Dewey was one of our most brilliant and courageous naval commanders. During the Spanish-American War of 1898, he navigated his fleet into Manila Bay despite the presence of mines in the water and huge guns firing from shore. Eventually troops disembarked from his ships and occupied the bay until the army could take over and make the victory complete.

Of course, we know that sailors and soldiers aren't the only ones who have to fight. Whether battling the enemy directly or skirting dangerous mines and ambushes, we, too, face conflicts, but not always with enemies! In fact, we often find ourselves in fights with those we love and respect. How will we deal with such conflicts in a way that brings honor and value to those we're confronting?

Navigate the Storms of Conflict!

That all of us will have conflict in our lives is inevitable. But I've heard it said that it's not the sugar that makes the tea sweet, it's the stirring. In other words, conflict can result in something good.

If we handle it right.

If we move through it with patience and wisdom.

So let's take some time to view the conflicts in our ministry lives. Let's begin to see them as opportunities to grow rather than just problems to solve. A friend of mine, Ed McGuigan, shared with me a unique, nautical way of naming our "response styles" when dealing with conflict. Below are his seven descriptions of the ways our attitudes surface when we face a relational storm. Each style is named for a type of ship that, for good or bad, can be used to navigate the seas of discord without being pulled under.

I. The Battleship Response

The battleship is the conqueror—built to fight and win.

Folks who use this response will not settle for a loss. They're the Admiral Deweys of the relationship skirmish. The Navy doesn't send battleships out into the water for the purpose of sinking them into the depths. No, those ships sail forward with all their big guns, all their heavy armor, ready to annihilate and conquer.

Ever had an argument with a battleship personality? These are the people who go into conflict to win; in fact, some of them actually *create* conflict (intentionally or unintentionally) because they are just built to fight. They like to argue, and they like to savor a verbal victory. When backed into a tight harbor—and loss seems imminent—they just bring out bigger and louder artillery. They may reach way into the past to bring up things to use against you. Anything goes to win this war.

➔**Fighting the waves in a battleship.** Imagine two children's ministry workers seated in the wheelhouse of the battleship, perhaps a man and a woman. Bob is a battleship responder and says, "Since I'm teaching the class, I'm choosing to use the curriculum from XYZ Company for my sixth-grade boys." Betty, who is chairperson of the Christian Education Committee, says, "But we wanted all the teachers to use our church's self-developed lessons plans."

In true battleship fashion, the man might say something like this, "You see this booklet? This is what I'm using this Sunday morning. Now, if you would like to teach the class yourself, then you can use any material you want." In other words, it's "my way or the highway." Or to stick with our sea-faring imagery, "Give way to my ego, or I'll torpedo." (I have not yet begun to fight.)

➔**A biblical example.** James and John, the sons of thunder: "When James and John, followers of Jesus, saw this, they said, 'Lord, do you want us to call fire down from heaven and destroy those people?'" (Luke 9:54, NCV). (When some Samaritans snubbed Jesus, these two disciples saw it as an attack that needed to be counterattacked immediately—with deadly force!)

2. The Submarine Response

The submarine is the deserter—built to disappear.

As soon as fighting begins to churn the surface waters, submariners push the "Dive! Dive! Dive!" button. *Ahhhhooooguh!*

They go under. They disappear—totally withdraw.

But please realize, this doesn't mean they don't want to win the conflict. As a matter of fact, they will often use their withdrawal and silence as a weapon to win the battle...eventually.

I would intentionally use this response during my first few years of marriage. It's not a matter of getting loud but of tactically deploying to gain the advantage. I'd go under, relocate, and come up from a different angle—and maybe even launch a couple of well-aimed torpedoes before going back under. I would always get the last word, of course, before diving out of sight to avoid a counterattack. It was very effective.

➜**Fighting the waves in a submarine.** How does this work for our ministry team members seated in the sub's sonar room? Well, let's say the woman is using the submarine response. The man says, "That's right, I'm using this curriculum if I'm going to have to teach this class."

What does she do? She shuts down. She doesn't have to physically leave the room, but she does refuse to fight (at least openly).

This can be OK, a good way to avoid a fight that may not be necessary, and to choose a more worthy battle should one arise in the future. In the submariner's mind, not every issue calls for "do or die," as with the battleship response. But beware: This type of responder is susceptible to making a passive-aggressive counterattack. What do I mean? Here's what could happen:

> ➜Betty places the order for the curriculum books, but "forgets" to order the Teacher's Guide;
> ➜Betty places the order for the books, but only gets enough for half of the students; or
> ➜Betty orders the books—to be delivered "C.O.D." to the teacher's door (rather than routinely billing the expense to the church).

The possibilities for stealthy torpedoing are endless. But I'm sure you get the idea. And even though choosing your battles *is* a good idea, continuing to fight them from the murky depths usually just escalates the hostilities.

➜**A biblical example.** Jonah: "But Jonah ran away from the Lord" (Jonah 1:3a). (Jonah's duty was to confront the Ninevites—something that would have been difficult and emotionally draining; he chose to "submerge" instead.)

3. The Aircraft Carrier Response

The aircraft carrier is the deployer—built to avoid engaging the enemy directly.

Similar to the submarine response, this style of conflict management goes a step further by deploying others to engage the enemy and then report back. Now aircraft carriers are not completely defenseless. They have small guns to assist them if they're under fire. However, their primary objective is to deploy others. They are set up to carry warriors and will rarely engage in a conflict directly.

I would venture to say that this is a favorite approach in churches in which people don't want to directly offer their critiques (or express their hurts, frustrations, or disappointments). Again, this can be perfectly acceptable, because even Jesus sent out his disciples to do some confronting on his behalf. However, in a warped application of this response, some people will deploy others but refuse to back them up or even acknowledge that they themselves were the original senders of the message. They will keep whispering to third parties until the criticism rises to the right people.

→**Fighting the waves on a carrier.** Our ministry duo is conversing up on the flight deck, and the woman is the aircraft-carrier responder. Here's how it goes:

He says, "I want to purchase this curriculum."

She responds by turning to three other team members hovering nearby and says to them, "Guys, we had decided to go with our own self-developed materials, right? Wasn't that the consensus at the June meeting? I'm wondering if Bob, here, may have missed that meeting?"

She may do this in Bob's hearing—or she may do it later, or the next day. Now the deck is rolling a bit, and lots of people know that Bob is trying to start a little "mutiny" with his own decision about curriculum. Eventually, Bob will hear that his decision isn't popular with "the rest of the team." But he wonders, "Who, exactly, am I quarreling with here?"

→**A biblical example.** Pilate to the crowd: "Pilate said, 'I have Barabbas and Jesus. Which do you want me to set free for you?' The people answered, 'Barabbas' " (Matthew 27:21, NCV). (In a classic aircraft carrier response, Pilate let someone else make the tough decision. The buck would not stop with him; let the crowd decide—no use engaging the Jesus case directly.)

4. The Canoe Response

The canoe is the negotiator—built for compromise and balance.

The person employing this style says, "I will only give something if I get something in return." In other words, I'll paddle on the right side, if you paddle just as hard on the left. I'll lean right if you'll lean left. But if you don't lean left, then I will just dump this whole thing right here.

There's no problem with this approach, provided both paddlers can reach a viable compromise. If not, there's potential for heading further into the white waters.

→**Fighting the waves in a canoe.** Attempting to do battle in a canoe is, obviously, a very tricky and delicate operation! Everyone involved can end up drenched—or drowned.

Let's take a look at Bob and Betty in the canoe. Let's say Bob is in the canoe, and Betty says, "I really think you ought to go with the committee's decision about your lesson materials, Bob."

Bob's likely response? Probably something along these lines: "I'll agree to use those materials this quarter, if you'll let me choose my own for the next quarter." The rest of the conversation will be a give-and-take bargaining session, with the canoer only satisfied when everything comes out "fair" or "even."

→A biblical example. Gideon: "Gideon said to God, 'If you will save Israel by my hand as you have promised—look, I will place a wool fleece on the threshing floor. If there is dew only on the fleece and all the ground is dry, then I will know that you will save Israel by my hand as you said'" (Judges 6:36-37). (Gideon's negotiating style comes through clearly here. He's basically saying, "God, I'll be happy to do your will, if you'll just prove to me that everything is going to work out OK.")

5. The Lifeboat Response

The lifeboat is the drifter—built to yield.

Lifeboat responders yield to whatever conflict is raging. These folks just hate confrontation, and they will do whatever it takes to get out of a conflict. They are powerless to set their own course, because they don't have an engine (and those little bitty oars don't do much good in a storm). So lifeboaters just go with the flow and hope that the storm will soon pass.

→Fighting the waves in a lifeboat. There are people who yield in every conflict, and this is certainly admirable—because Jesus did say to "turn the other cheek." In our ministry conflict situation, Betty the CE committee chairwoman, is the lifeboater and says, "I was really hoping you'd use our curriculum like all the other teachers, but if you really want to use this book, then go ahead."

> We can bury emotion, but we never bury it dead.

What is the problem with this type of response? Unfortunately, the lifeboater not only may turn her cheek but also may play the martyr's role in the relationship—and play it for all it's worth. (Even this can be a subtle ploy to get one's way.)

If she keeps "stuffing" her anger about the situation, she'll also get depressed—or eventually explode in rage (remember, some life rafts are made of air-filled rubber). We can bury emotion, but we never bury it dead. We always bury our anger alive, and it will "rise up" on some future day, usually when least expected.

Not a pretty sight.

→A biblical example. Peter: "A servant girl saw Peter sitting there in the firelight, and looking closely at him, she said, 'This man was also with him.' But Peter said this was not true; he said, 'Woman, I don't know him'" (Luke 22:56-57, NCV).

6. The Fireboat Response

The fireboat is the extinguisher—built to put out fires.

Like the others, this style isn't altogether bad, but it isn't altogether good, either. The fireboater turns on the water cannons at the first sign of smoke. He tries to fix everything with quick solutions.

→Fighting the waves in a fireboat. When our ministry colleagues are out on the waters of conflict, Betty, if she's the fireboater, may try to defuse the conflict before it ever begins. She may say something like this: "I sure hope you aren't thinking about choosing your own curriculum, Bob. We've tried allowing that, awhile back, and things

(honor)

just didn't work out. Anyway, I know you're just going to love what we've developed, and once you try it, I'm quite sure you'll see its benefits. And the kids seem to take to it, as well. In fact, I was talking to one of the other teachers, and she agreed that..."

The person with the fireboat response wants to stop the conflict before it even starts and gets burning out of control. Yet sometimes conflicts need to be aired, expressed, and then resolved. In fact, when it comes to conflict in interpersonal relationships—as in major surgery—sometimes things have to get worse (get *cut open!*) before they can get better. In most cases, it's best to *move through* conflict rather than try to avoid it.

→**A biblical example.** Barnabas: "Barnabas wanted to take John Mark with them, but he had left them at Pamphylia; he did not continue with them in the work. So Paul did not think it was a good idea to take him. Paul and Barnabas had such a serious argument about this that they separated and went different ways. Barnabas took Mark and sailed to Cyprus" (Acts 15:37-39 NCV). (Paul and Barnabas could have continued to seek dialogue after their big argument. They could have ended up working together in ministry for years to come. Instead, they used a fireboat style and avoided any other fights down the road.)

7. The Tugboat Response

The tugboat is the rescuer—built to solve problems.

The tugboater constantly seeks resolution. He or she says, "We can overcome any problem if we both cooperate." This person determines not to fuel the conflict, doesn't try to avoid the conflict, doesn't try to dowse the conflict with water, and doesn't ignore the conflict. Rather he or she *engages* the conflict with a single-minded commitment to bringing about a solution.

→**Calming the waves in a tugboat**. In our ministry conflict situation, Bob and Betty are chugging along, discussing the curriculum conflict. She says, "Well, why don't we do this? Suppose you come to our next meeting and do a presentation on the curriculum you'd like to use with your sixth-grade boys? Tell us all about it, and show us why you're so enthused about it. I'm pretty sure we'll be willing to take a close look at it. And maybe if it's not right for this quarter, we could start a separate elective class where the kids who want to study a different course could sign up for it as an alternative. Who knows? I'm sure we'll find a creative solution in which everybody wins."

This, of course, is the highest and best response to conflict. It's a win-win situation. But are the other responses always wrong? No, there are times we should take one of these vessels during the heat of conflict. In fact, Jesus employed every one of these styles throughout his ministry:

→**Battleship:** When Jesus cleansed the temple, Matthew 21:12.
→**Submarine:** When Jesus walked through the midst of the crowd and departed, Luke 4:29.
→**Aircraft carrier:** When Jesus sent out the twelve, Matthew 10:5.
→**Canoe:** When Jesus used help feeding the five thousand with five loaves and two fish, Matthew 14:17-19.

→**Lifeboat:** When Jesus didn't answer before the high priest, Matthew 26:62-63.

→**Fireboat:** When Jesus engaged the disciples over who was the greatest in the kingdom, Luke 22:24-26.

→**Tugboat:** When Jesus said, "and whoever comes to me, I will never drive away," John 6:37b.

So each of the boat styles can have its appropriate place in our conflict-management armada. But we must choose wisely, in each situation, which boat will take us to peaceful shores in the most God-honoring way. Normally, we will first seek to use the tugboat.

Finally, I'd like to point out: Not only do boats run into rough navigating, planes can get hit, too. The Los Angeles Times on June 10, 1988, displayed this interesting headline:

$16 Million Jet Fighter Destroyed in Florida Collision With Wild Pigs [1]

I'm going to recount this article here to set the stage for talking about how we need to *act our way into honoring*—and things that can disrupt that for us.

> How many of us will let our valuable lives end up in the trees because we refuse to deal with the conflicts—the wild pigs—that shuffle down our runway of life?

A pair of wild pigs that wandered off course were hit by an F-16 fighter, forcing the pilot to eject as the jet veered off a runway and crashed at Jacksonville International Airport yesterday. The pigs were killed, the pilot was bruised, and the $16 million jet was destroyed. Lieutenant Colonel Sam Carter, age 46, was rolling down the runway at 160 mph after landing Tuesday night, when he saw a brown blur and felt a bump before his National Guard jet veered toward a ditch and into a stand of pine trees.

Carter, who has flown jets for more than twenty-four years, including sorties over Vietnam, ejected before the aircraft plowed into the woods. "It is a very inglorious way for a $16 million aircraft to come to an end," Carter said, who was bruised, but otherwise uninjured. It was the first time he had ever bailed out of an aircraft. The rocket-powered ejection seat carried Carter two-hundred feet into the air, barely high enough for his parachute to open. Carter said the chute blossomed just before his feet hit the ground. Colonel Don Garrett, commanding officer of the Florida Air National Guards 125th Fighter Interceptor Group, said that the pigs must have been struck by the plane's left landing gear as Carter was landing.

How many of us will let our valuable lives end up in the trees because we refuse to deal with the conflicts—the wild pigs—that shuffle down our runway of life? Don't let

How to Foster Accountability

As ministry leaders, we need to take positive action to encourage helpful and healthy accountability. Here are four ways to proceed:[2]

1. **Welcome it.** We can work to avoid being defensive when people offer suggestions, maintaining an open ear for feedback. When we protect ourselves with defense mechanisms, we become hard, which is too steep a price to pay. Think the following questions over:
   → How do I typically handle "suggestions"?
   → When have I been defensive lately?
   → What is my favorite defense mechanism?

2. **Model it.** Holding others accountable requires a willingness to confront others with some difficult truths, and with love. At the same time, it models to others how they can hold us accountable as leaders. Think the following questions over:
   → Am I willing to confront in love?
   → What kinds of modeling am I doing in this area?

3. **Use opportunities to teach about accountability.** We can talk about what we are doing and why—what principles are guiding the confrontation. Jesus used conflict and misunderstandings as a well-lit stage for instruction. Think the following questions over:
   → What have I taught about accountability here?
   → Am I aware of the biblical principles that call Christians to mutual accountability?
   → How can a recent conflict act as a catalyst for increasing the practice of accountability in this ministry?

4. **Never question people's motives.** Accusations are like chemical weapons: They poison the atmosphere. When we wonder what's driving others, we can say, "I may be wrong, but it looks to me that so and so happened. Tell me how you're feeling about it." When we refuse to question others' motives, they are less likely to question ours. Think the following questions over:
   → Do I tend to accuse others—even inadvertently?
   → Have I learned to tactfully question others' intentions, always assuming the best?
   → How good are my listening skills?

the little piggies in your life wreck a valuable relationship or an honoring relationship. Instead, take personal responsibility for the health of your relationships and your team. One of the best ways to do this is to foster a spirit of mutual accountability.

Be Accountable to One Another!

We do have a responsibility to the others on our ministry teams. Let's say you have a team of three or four people. Do you have their phone numbers? Do you have their addresses? Let's say that Kristin, Cathy, and Anne are a team. One day, Kristin just doesn't show up in the class. Then Cathy says to Anne, "Where's Kristin?"

"I don't know."

Well, if you communicate during the week, you're accountable to each other about when you're going to get there and who's carrying what load. Can you imagine the smoothness of going into that morning and being effective in ministering to our kids when that happens? That's the process of accountability.

During World War II, a plant of parachute packers achieved extreme notoriety. The reason was that their parachutes only opened nineteen out of twenty times! That's an average of 95 percent, and that's a great percentage if you're taking a test in school, or shooting free throws in the NBA. But when you're jumping out of a plane, that's just not good enough. So the manager of the plant developed a strategy to increase reliability. *He required the packers first to test the parachutes themselves.* It wasn't long before quality rose to 100 percent. That's the principle of accountability at work—taking personal responsibility for the successful functioning of the team.

Yet we can be hindered from doing so. In fact, I came up with some distractions, or hindrances, to mutual accountability that you may have noticed also plaguing you or others on your team lately:

Arrogance

In relation to teamwork, this means having a personal agenda without paying attention to anyone else's agenda. The Bible says God opposes the proud but gives grace to the humble. We're called to defer to one another in honor, and that helps to maintain a dynamic team. The key question to ask yourself in this regard is, *Do I use power or earn authority?* I was present at a staff meeting several years ago in which the person in charge of a particular group said, "I need and demand your respect." But respect and authority are *earned* over time. Power and control are demanded immediately. Remember this: If you have to tell someone who you are, then maybe you aren't.

Rugged Individualism

How is this different from arrogance? There are certain professional athletes who say, "You know what? I'm not going to show up for that team meeting." By their actions, they're saying, "I'm more valuable than the team." When you're part of a team, you have to make personal sacrifices on many levels. Certainly, not showing up for things is a way of saying, "I'm just not getting anything here, and I would rather not show up. It's all about meeting *my* needs." We really can't do that if we're going to remain a team. "All of us" are smarter and stronger than "one of us." There is no "I" in T-E-A-M!

> End runs are probably the single greatest cause of breaking trust in teams.

Lack of Loyalty, Lack of Support

Have you said, "I'm not going to be loyal to that"? Or do you participate in activities outside of the team that would bring down other team members? that is, talking about other team members in a discouraging light? agreeing to something at a team meeting, but bad-mouthing the idea later? Now you have the idea.

End Runs

This is going around, under, or above the organizational structure. In the business world, it's when your boss does something you don't like and you don't go directly to him about it. You go around him and talk to his boss. That's deplorable. Scripture says that if you have difficulty with someone, you go to that person. End runs are probably the single greatest cause of breaking trust in teams. We need to go directly to the source and say, "How can we work this out?"

Join the Honor Parade

In his book *Waking From the American Dream*, Don McCullough wrote that during World War II, Winston Churchill called together the labor leaders in Great Britain and told them there was a great need to increase coal production. He gave them the facts, tried to enlist their support, and then concluded his presentation by telling them he was sure that after the war there would be a parade in Piccadilly Circus.

> First, [Churchill] said, would come the sailors who had kept the vital sea lanes open. Then would come the soldiers who had come home from Dunkirk and then gone on to defeat Rommel in Africa. Then would come the pilots who had driven the Luftwaffe from the sky.
>
> Last of all, he said, would come a long line of sweat-stained, soot-streaked men in miner's caps. Someone would cry from the crowd, "And where were you during the critical days of our struggle?" And from ten thousand throats would come the answer, "We were deep in the earth with our faces to the coal."[3]

May I suggest another parade for you? It's a parade led by our King of kings and Lord of lords. And with him will be the men and women of the Old Testament who gave us unswerving examples of faith. With them will be the men and women of the New Testament who, through their great perseverance, made Christ known. And with them will be the men and women who serve as missionaries in foreign lands, sacrificing all to share Christ.

And then, last of all, will come a long line of sweat-stained men and women. And on that day, if someone should shout from the crowd, "And where were you during the critical days of our struggle to advance the kingdom?" from deep within thousands of throats will spring the reply, *"We were leading the children, and our faces were in his Word."*

For Reflection and Discussion

1. How do you define "successful conflict resolution"?

2. Talk about this in your ministry team: *How do we tend to handle conflict around here?* (Just listen to each person's point of view, without interruption.)

3. Give each person in your group the opportunity to identify the "type of boat" he or she usually rides into rough waters. Let other group members agree or disagree—and tell *why*.

4. Why is mutual accountability so important to honoring one another? How has your team practiced accountability in the past?

Endnotes

1. "$16 Million Jet Fighter Destroyed in Florida Collision With Wild Pigs," Los Angeles Times (June 10, 1988).

2. These four ways to foster accountability are adapted from Paul A. Cedar in James D. Berkley, ed., *Leadership Handbooks of Practical Theology, Volume 3: Leadership and Administration* (Grand Rapids: Baker Books, 1994), 9.

3. The Winston Churchill story was retold on the Internet at http://groups.yahoo.com/group/mydailydose/message/120, accessed September 13, 2001.

TWELVE

→Honoring Yourself: First Step to Honoring Others

"I seem to be racing around more than ever—but getting farther and farther behind!"

I'm sure you've heard something like that recently—or said it yourself! We're familiar with that concept, aren't we? Most of us feel as if we have to run at warp speed just to get a few small things accomplished during a day. In fact, our lives seem always to be picking up speed—but quickly moving us into burnout.

Have you noticed that it's always "Hurry up and slow down"? It really should be "Just slow down."

That's what I'd like to try to walk you through—the art of honoring yourself so that you can honor others more effectively. We're going to talk about purposes, priorities, time management, and downtime as ways to honor yourself (which is something God wants you to do). If you're the type of person who wakes up each morning and thinks, "Hey! I won't have enough time to get everything done today," this is the topic for you. Let me just tell you upfront that I am not the authority on avoiding burnout. So I'm going to be learning right along with you to put burnout on the back burner.

How to Put Out Burnout

Isaiah 49:4 basically says, "I've worked hard all my life for nothing. I've used all my energies, but I've accomplished nothing useful." If you're anything like me, I've sat at the end of the day and shuffled some piles around on my desk and said, "What did I accomplish today? Did I influence anything at all? Did I make any life-changing impact?"

> Burnout is less a matter of being too busy than a matter of having nothing truly *significant* to be busy *about.*

Those kinds of feelings can eventually lead to burnout, because burnout is less a matter of being too busy than a matter of having nothing truly *significant* to be busy *about.* What can you do to reverse the flow and start getting built up? Let's look at five actions you can begin taking right now.

I. Initialize the Firebreak Around Your Life.

A good friend of mine is a fire captain in town. He's been on the firefighting force for years, and not too long ago I actually saw him and his team fighting a brush fire. When they pulled up on the scene, they didn't immediately attack the fire; instead, they circled around it. Using some shovels and other earth-moving equipment, they began to cut what's called a "firebreak." They finished that and stepped back, even though this fire was burning out of control. When I asked what they were doing, he said they were waiting for the fire to reach the firebreak. When the fire reaches that area, it burns itself out.

Likewise, it's hard to attack a burning-out-of-control life. Some of us need to sit down this week and cut a firebreak around our lives. Specifically, that means setting aside a time of solitude—with no VCR, no CD, no cell phone—and saying, "Who am I, really? How is my relationship with my Lord these days? And what is the overriding purpose in my life?"

2. Realize Your Purpose in Life.

Each one of us was designed on purpose. Ephesians 5:15 says: "Be very careful, then, how you live—not as unwise but as wise." So we need to take an inventory of where we think God is calling us. Matthew 20:26-28 says, "Whoever wants to become great among you must be your servant, and whoever wants to be first must be your slave—just as the Son of Man did not come to be served, but to serve, and to give his life as a ransom for many." Clearly, as a part of our purpose in life, *God has designed us to serve others as a key component of our life mission.*

When I was in college, one of the students gave a talk in my Philosophy of Ministry class. He handed out some little cards that displayed this poem:

> *Here lie the bones of Nancy Jones.*
> *Her life held no terrors.*
> *She lived an old maid,*
> *She died an old maid;*
> *No hits, no runs, no errors.*

(honor)

> We walk through life merely *preparing* to live, while staying very safe and secure behind certain self-imposed boundaries.

That stuck with me because sometimes I think we walk through life merely *preparing* to live, while staying very safe and secure behind certain self-imposed boundaries. But God may be calling you to adventure—right now!

Obviously, if we want to make a life-changing impact, we'll need to do more than just "make a living." So we have to realize our purpose. We all have 168 hours per week, and it's up to us to choose how to use those hours. So I ask you, how are you investing those hours? family time, work time, career time, church time, serving? We can get burned out if we fail to focus those hours for the things that truly matter.

I was reading through an article about an interview with Zig Ziglar, the great motivator. The title was "Only the Thankful Can Burn Brightly Without Burning Out." Here's what Ziglar says:

God hasn't promised me five more minutes, but at 71, I honestly believe I'm at least ten, maybe fifteen, years away from hitting my peak. I believe my career's in front of me, though if God decides my life is over today, I'm ready.

My creativity today is substantially better than it was 25 years ago. My energy level is higher than when I was 45...I'm also better organized than I was 25 years ago. I schedule exercise time, eat sensibly, and I normally get about seven-and-a-half hours of sleep.[1]

As I read Ziglar's words, they reminded me that "it's what you learn after you 'know it all' that counts." Here's a guy who's seventy-one, and he's saying he's still years away from hitting his peak. For those of us involved in the ministry, we might put it like this: "Hey, we're making an impact. We know where we're going; God is leading us there; we have yet to fully live out our purpose in God's kingdom."

3. Prioritize Your Key Life Areas.

Don't necessarily make a to-do list, because those to-do lists never go away. John Maxwell says we should simply ask, "What gives me the greatest return?"

Here's where the Paretto Principle comes into play (also known as the 80-20 Rule). Paretto was an Italian economist who came up with a concept that says: If I were to ask you to write ten things that make your life successful, then I would suggest to you that two of those things (or 20 percent of those ten things) give you 80 percent of your results. Eight of those things give you only 20 percent of your results.

If you use the Paretto Principle and write the top ten things you think you're being called to do in prioritizing our lives, then I would say that two of those things on your list are giving you the greatest reward and return of your life.

A Personal Goal-Setting Snapshot

Here's an example of what I have set up for my own goal structure—the six areas for me:

1. Spiritual growth goals. This would be quiet times, journaling time, and prayer time.

2. Family growth goals. Family goals help me focus on being a better parent and a better husband. We have passes to several entertainment facilities within our community for the sake of building family time. We have passes to the zoo and the aquarium. Our kids like these places, and we can drive to both of them within an hour. We have a great time in the car, and we can go spontaneously. Occasionally, I will just come home and say, "Let's go to the aquarium!"

My wife and I regularly have a date night, usually on Friday evenings, even if only for an hour or two. We get away to have some Mommy and Daddy time to be better parents, and better spouses.

3. Leadership growth goals. For myself, I list twelve different books to read, one per month. I listen to a certain number of audiotapes and stay up-to-date on ministry trends through reading various periodicals. I also attempt to learn what Web sites are popular with kids, so I can relate and program better in this new century.

4. Physical growth goals. I'm aware that I need to eat right and exercise to stay healthy and keep my mind focused. I thoroughly enjoy hockey, so I play on a team a couple of times a week. (It's also the only game a pastor can play that allows him to "hit" people! I really like to play after budget meetings.)

5. Professional growth goals. We can't become what we need to be by remaining what we are. So with that in mind, we need professional goals to advance in our vocation. These goals might involve studying communication or maybe taking a computer class or a graphics course. What are you doing in your workplace? I'm working on vision casting, building children, developing and overseeing projects, and mentoring leaders.

6. Personal growth goals. Scheduling vacation time, taking a day off, looking for someone to build into and mentor me—these are all areas in which I strive to stay focused and grow personally. I also develop hobby-related goals, such as shaving a few strokes off the golf score. These things provide that balance between life and ministry.

Every year in August, I sit down and I say, "What am I going to do this coming year in these areas?" I'll tell you this: If you're not writing your goals, you're hitting them every time. Why not take some time right now to jot some of your own goals?

So instead of making a to-do list, find out which 20 percent is giving you that 80 percent return, *and do more of that*, instead of doing the 80 percent that only gives you a small return. In other words, focus more on a goal list than on a to-do list.

4. Maximize Your Time.

Paul said in Ephesians 5:17, "Do not be foolish, but understand what the Lord's will is." That's a great reminder on planning and organizing our time. I always say, "If you fail to plan, you plan to fail."

But when I say "maximizing," I'm talking about something that goes the next step beyond just organizing and planning. Ecclesiastes 11:4 says, "Whoever watches the wind will not plant; whoever looks at the clouds will not reap." In other words, if you wait for absolutely perfect conditions, you'll never get anything done. So we need to make sure that we maximize our time and gain some time back during the day. Here are some of my favorite ways to do it:

➡Don't put it down, put it away.

When you get all the stuff in the mail, stand right there over the trash can and throw away everything you don't need, and then walk over to the file drawer and put your bills in your "bills to be paid" file. It's a "clean as you go" principle. *Don't pile it, file it.*

> Surprisingly, the deeper into a task we go, the more our attitude is likely to become more positive. On the other hand, if we wait for our feelings to change, we may never get started at all.

➡Do it now.

The reason we don't do it now is we don't like to do what we need to do now! We just keep putting it off. Our emotions dictate our actions. But try this amazingly effective reversal: *Act your way into feeling, don't feel your way into acting.* Just take the first step when a difficult task faces you, regardless of your negative feelings about it. After that, take the next small step, and then the next… Surprisingly, the deeper into a task we go, the more our attitude is likely to become more positive. On the other hand, if we wait for our feelings to change, we may never get started at all.

➡Finish one thing before starting another.

If you're like me, you've got twenty-three irons in the fire and none of them get very hot. Start with one thing, do it well, and bring it to completion. A key technique here is simply to *get started*, especially when you feel overwhelmed by all that needs to be done. Just learn to break large tasks into smaller subtasks so you can slowly get your project off the ground.

➡Use waiting time.

We want to be effective and efficient. Effectiveness is doing the right things, and efficiency is doing things right. If you're getting your oil changed, bring something to read. Or use waiting time to listen to audiotapes in the car. Or make use of downtime by letting yourself just rest.

→Invest in tools that will help you get your job done.

I brought a little tool to a speaking engagement to illustrate this point. It was a digital voice recorder. Do you have one? Some people will say that it just creates more work. But I get ideas in weird places: the shower, the mall, the car, wherever. I just push a button and throw the idea into the recorder. Anyone can have ideas, but it's the person who writes them and pursues them who is successful.

→Understand your personality.

Don't hang around people who continually drain you. If they keep usurping all of your energy, pretty soon you get washed up. So ask yourself: Am I an introvert or an extrovert? I am a pretty solid introvert. Being around a lot of people for an extended period of time drains me. I know that. So I remove myself for times of solitude so that I can get re-energized or "built into." If you're an extrovert, being around people may energize you. Understand who you are, and then pursue what nurtures your spirit.

→Plan your day the night before.

Get your clothes ready and gather materials for meetings. Do what it takes *before* you have to rush around searching for your socks! This is a matter of determining to control the flow in your own life.

5. Energize Yourself With Downtime.

This is my favorite, because I enjoy vacations and I enjoy renewing my ministry batteries. Sadly, I rarely plan for downtime.

Did you know that according to some researchers, about half of all physical problems are stress-related? Think about all the headaches, backaches, and stomach and digestive problems that doctors try to treat every day. Imagine how many of them could be cured if folks would simply do a better job of handling their daily stresses.

Rest is not a sin. It's a requirement. So schedule rest and recreation times. If you're married, schedule "date nights" away from the kids. Do something that builds you up and replenishes you. Sometimes we need to just shut down and get re-energized. My wife and I enjoy going to hockey games. We talk in the car on the way there, and at the game we enjoy screaming our lungs out (very therapeutic!).

How Will You Fit the Rocks?

A few years ago, I read about an interesting time-management expert. He was speaking to a group of business students, and to drive home his point, he used an illustration that the students would never forget. He stood in front of this group of high-powered overachievers and said, "OK, it's time for a quick quiz." He pulled out a gallon-size, wide-mouthed Mason jar and set it on the table in front of them. Then he took out about twelve fist-sized rocks and carefully placed each one into the jar, until there was no more room. He asked, "Is this jar full?"

Everyone answered, "Yes."

"Are you sure? Is it really full?"

He waited for a moment, and then reached under the table and pulled out a bucket

(honor)

of gravel. He dumped some gravel into the jar, shook the jar, and let the gravel pieces work themselves down in between the rocks. "Is this jar full?"

The class answered, "Well, probably not."

He nodded in agreement. He reached under the table again and pulled out a bucket of sand. He started dumping the sand into the jar. When all the spaces in the jar were seemingly filled, he asked again if the jar was full.

This time the whole class shouted, "No!"

Once again, he agreed. He grabbed a pitcher of water and began to pour it into the jar until it was filled to the brim. Then he looked up at the class and asked, "What is the point of this illustration?"

One eager young man raised his hand and said, "The point is, no matter how full your schedule is, if you try really hard, you can always fit some more things into it."

The speaker said, "No, that's not the point. The truth that this illustration teaches us is this: *If you don't put the big rocks in first, you will never get them in at all.*"

So the question for you today is, What are the big rocks in your life? Is it a project you want to accomplish? Is it more time with your spouse or your kids? Is it your education? your finances? Is it your time at church? your impact for Christ? Make sure what's truly important goes in first. The rest will take care of itself.

When we are truly overloaded in life, we have a tendency to dishonor others; *we simply don't have room for them.* A healthy self is the first step to making healthy choices, which leads to healthy, honoring relationships.

If you want to have a successful, thriving ministry to children, then you need to lead effectively. Vision, mission, values, and goals are just a few of the foundational pieces that must be in place for healthy growth to occur. The intangibles, which are rarely taught at the university or in seminary, are some of the most important things you'll need to lead your children's ministry. Concepts like sustaining passion, choosing the right attitude, developing a great team, and showing honor are hard to put your arms around. My hope and prayer, as I pen these final words, is that you will, for the rest of your ministry, live your life pleasing to the Lord and make a firm commitment to lead yourself and others on the right PATH.

For Reflection and Discussion

1. Name some of the "hurried" aspects of your life these days. What would help you slow down a bit?

2. This week just pause and assess the "fire of the urgent" in your life. How will you begin to cut a break around the urgent this week?

3. Write out a simple purpose statement for your life. Why are you here?

4. How can you tell when you're hovering on the brink of burnout? What are the signs you watch for in your ministry colleagues?

5. Which of the time-maximizing suggestions could help you most? What could you do to implement them in the days ahead?

Endnote

1. Zig Ziglar interview in "More Oxygen to the Flame," Leadership Journal, Fall 1998.

Group Publishing, Inc.
Attention: Product Development
P.O. Box 481
Loveland, CO 80539
Fax: (970) 679-4370

Evaluation of
Leadership Essentials for Children's Ministry

Please help Group Publishing, Inc. continue to provide innovative and useful resources for ministry. Please take a moment to fill out this evaluation and mail or fax it to us. Thanks!

● ● ●

1. As a whole, this book has been (circle one)

not very helpful   very helpful

1   2   3   4   5   6   7   8   9   10

2. The best things about this book:

3. Ways this book could be improved:

4. Things I will change because of this book:

5. Other books I'd like to see Group publish in the future:

6. Would you be interested in field-testing future Group products and giving us your feedback? If so, please fill in the information below:

Name _____

Church Name _____

Denomination _____ Church Size _____

Church Address _____

City _____ State _____ ZIP _____

Church Phone _____

E-mail _____

Flagship church resources

from Group Publishing

Innovations From Leading Churches

Flagship Church Resources are your shortcut to innovative and effective leadership ideas. You'll find ideas for every area of church leadership including pastoral ministry, adult ministry, youth ministry, and children's ministry.

Flagship Church Resources are created by the leaders of thriving, dynamic, and trend-setting churches around the country. These nationally recognized teaching churches host regional leadership conferences and are respected by other pastors and church leaders because their approaches to ministry are so effective. These flagship church resources reveal the proven ideas, programs, and principles that these churches have put into practice.

Flagship Church Resources currently available:

- *Doing Life With God*
- *Doing Life With God 2*
- *The Visual Edge:*
  Compelling Video Connectors for Your Worship Experience
- *Mission-Driven Worship:*
  Helping Your Changing Church Celebrate God
- *An Unstoppable Force:*
  Daring to Become the Church God Had in Mind
- *A Follower's Life:*
  12 Group Studies on What It Means to Walk With Jesus
- *Leadership Essentials for Children's Ministry*
- *Keeping Your Head Above Water:*
  Refreshing Insights for Church Leadership
- *Seeing Beyond Church Walls:*
  Action Plans for Touching Your Community
- *unLearning Church:*
  Just When You Thought You Had Leadership All Figured Out!

With more to follow!